Burnt Out

A Paramedic's Memoir

By Chad Davis

DORRANCE
PUBLISHING CO
EST. 1920
PITTSBURGH, PENNSYLVANIA 15238

Dorrance Publishing Co
585 Alpha Drive
Suite 103
Pittsburgh, PA 15238
Visit our website at *www.dorrancebookstore.com*

ISBN: 979-8-88729-319-6
eISBN: 979-8-88729-819-1

*"I'm really, really, really tired of people calling it burnout. What over 50% of health care professionals are experiencing, they call it burnout. It's exhaustion, low productivity, and a feeling of deep cynicism, and it's so prevalent that everyone, even in administration is starting to panic. Like 'What's going on? Why are physicians and nurses and PA's burning out?' Burnout is a kind of victim shaming. It's saying you're not resourceful enough, you're not resilient enough, you're not strong enough to adapt to a system, so maybe you should meditate. Maybe you should use some lavender essential oil, maybe we could have a wellness retreat, or hire a chief wellness officer! It's all bull sh*t! Here's what's really going on. We're not suffering from burnout. We're suffering from something that Wendy Dean and Simon Talbot called 'moral injury.' Let that sink in for a second. People go to war. They have a set of moral values. They care about other human beings, and then they're forced to either become a part of or bear witness to things that are so against everything they believe, and when they come back, they fall apart. We call it PTSD. We have a million different names for it. What it is, is **moral injury**. Humans are moral, idealistic creatures that resonate love for other humans, and what happens when our moral ideals meet the real world where we cannot give our patients the care that we know we could give if we have the tools and the resources and the autonomy to do it? What happens when we're trained in our schooling to give the best possible care to patients regardless of their socioeconomic status, regardless of their race, regardless of their condition, or their gender, but then we meet the real world where it's all about the insurance company's bottom line? It's all about the hospital system's revenue, it's all about throughput and RVUs, and then we meet an electronic health record that is a glorified cash register with little patient stuff tacked on? We stare at that instead of staring at the vulnerable person who's having the worst day of their lives and you can't be with them. How would that make anybody feel? Let alone some of the most resourceful, resilient,*

passionate human beings on the planet; our health care professionals. These are people who went into this field with an almost evangelical, religious zeal to help others. Why do I say that? Because they sacrificed their 20s, they sacrificed financial stability early on, they sacrificed family, they sacrificed sleep, and they sacrificed their own health, **because they felt they were going to be part of something much larger than them!** *That is the highest aspiration of any human being. They had a moral code to go with. Then, they meet our health care system and all it is is the opposite of what their morality tells them they need to do for patients. So, what's going to happen? What's going to happen to a good person in a bad system when they feel they can't change the system and they have to adapt. They're going to adapt, and adapt, and adapt...and then they're going to break, and that's what they call burnout. It's not burnout. The next administrator who tells you they're trying to manage burnout, tell them to go f*ck themselves. Tell them it's moral injury and until we know what it is, we're never going to be able to treat it. How are you going to treat moral injury? You change the system that is causing the moral injury. You change the electronic health record to make it about bringing us closer to our patients, about making eye contact, about taking busywork off our plate. You change the conflict that drives us. Any given doctor on any given day serves three masters, at least: the patient themselves and their family, their own financial interests, and their employer. All three of those may be at odds, so how do you fix moral injury? You bring them in sync. We should be able to do well financially and well with our families, and have time with our families while doing good for our patients. We call that healthcare 3.0 and it's where healthcare has to go. It means we need technology that enables the human relationship, that allows us to take care of the unique human story at hand. We need the tools, resources, and autonomy to do our jobs, because guess what? Administrators don't know how to take care of patients. That's why we exist. Why do you think they call health care workers that are actually touching patients 'frontline health care workers?' Where does that come from? Frontlines of war! We use the language of war when we're taking care of patients, and we suffer the wounds of war; the moral injury. That PTSD of not being able to live up to our ideals. So, the call to action is this. We on the front lines need to stand up to our leaders and demand that they lead, that they recognize that moral injury is something that needs to be taken into account, and we need to design systems and human systems that actually address that fundamental conflict. Stop putting band aids on burnout and victim shaming suffering* *clinicians who are committing suicide at alarming rates. If you think this is a victimless problem and doctors and nurses are just entitled, privileged whiners, you can shut the f*ck up because people are dying. Good people, friends of mine, friends of yours, have died from moral injury. It is not us. It is this system, and it's time that we fixed it."*

-Dr. Zubin Damania
"ZDoggMD"

PROLOGUE

"You should write a book."

For almost two decades, I have heard this statement more times than I can count. I have always considered myself a gifted writer, but the suggestion that I should put my stories to paper has always been more than a little silly to me. A book should tell a story, and a story about EMS plays more like a sitcom than a soap opera. From one call to the next, there is no common theme, so my book would read like a collection of short stories, which was something that had little appeal to me.

I had never been able to figure out how I could connect these unrelated events until I had an epiphany. Through the decades of toiling away in the back of an ambulance, from each call to each character, there was one commonality that I had not recognized. Me. After realizing that I was the commonality that links the stories, I still didn't know if I had a book. I wondered if I had a story worth telling, that I would want to read. Why would anyone want to read about me? But then there was that suggestion again, "You should write a book." *Maybe I should*, I thought.

"Begin with the end in mind." After months of self-examination, I came to believe that it was a ridiculous notion. My story had no end. I was neither dead nor retired, so there was no logical conclusion to the book. I put it in my back pocket and stowed the idea away for "one day." It was not until a job that I once loved became a chore that I began to examine my motivations. *How did I get here?* I asked myself.

I began writing as a therapeutic outlet and a way to process my own thoughts, but as the words flowed from my brain to my fingertips, my story began to come to life. It had a beginning and an end, a main character, supporting hero guides, and insight that surprised even me. My story was worth telling and revealed the journey that I took from a zealous young EMT to a weathered, burnt out paramedic.

People have an inherent curiosity about my job, and while I can tell the stories in all their guts and glory, the pieces that are not conveyed are usually my thoughts and feelings, how I process them, and how they have shaped me over the long haul. The stories provide an anecdotal insight, but the *saga*—man, what a ride.

My name is Chad Davis, and I have held the career that is the dream of little boys throughout the world. I am a firefighter/paramedic. I have served proudly with the Moyock, North Carolina Volunteer Fire Department, Currituck County, North Carolina Volunteer EMS, Portsmouth, Virginia Fire Department, Isle of Wight County, Virginia Department of Emergency Services, and with the Pike Township Fire Department in Indianapolis, Indiana, as well as a smattering of other small towns, stations, and companies along the way.

With the title of paramedic comes a set of cliché responses that every new acquaintance says upon learning of my profession. "You're a paramedic? I bet you see some crazy shit!" "I could never do what you do. I can't stand the sight of blood." And every medic's favorite, "What's the worst thing you've seen?" Often they want to show me their rash or ask for a diagnosis for an ache or pain that they've been having. The title "paramedic" comes with instant trust placed in you by complete strangers that would take years to earn in any other setting. People have little reservation or fear of sharing too much when they learn that you are in healthcare.

There was a time in my life when I delighted in the esteem placed on me, and I eagerly answered their questions, using it as an opportunity to bolster their opinion of me, but as the years have worn on, the allure of recognition has faded, and my responses are shorter and much less grotesque. In general, I attempt to fade into the crowd. When people ask what I do, I simply say, "I'm in healthcare," to avoid the dreaded "worst call" question. And if they figure it out and ask anyway, most of the time I simply respond with an extremely vanilla, "I'm not sure."

When people ask those questions, often they don't really want the real answers, and they could never understand my "matter of fact" way of retelling the story. My face doesn't match their level of shock, and there is nowhere to take the conversation from there. Nevertheless, they ask, and I get it. There was a time when I also hung on these stories, and a time when I wasn't sure that I could do this job either.

My first experience with blood came in my emergency room rotation as an EMT student. The student's job in this setting is mainly to assist nurses with making beds and distributing blankets to patients. You're a lowly observer, but if you do those two jobs well, you just might get called into a room to observe something interesting. My first rotation was at Albemarle Hospital in Elizabeth City, North Carolina, and I was called into a room to observe a suturing procedure. I was fascinated with the intricate process of drawing the sutures around the hemostats, and then pulling them tight before reversing direction and doing it the other way.

As I watched the doctor draw the needle through the skin and pull the wound closed, a wave of nausea began to wash over me. With each pass of the thread through the jagged edges of the wound, the waves of queasiness smacked me harder, and my vision began to narrow. I began to rock back and forth and then, WHAM! I passed out. A few moments later, I woke up in a hospital bed, feet in the air, with an amused nurse standing over me laughing. "Don't like the sight of blood, huh? Might want to find a different career."

This process repeated on two other occasions. Once on the scene of a decapitation, of which I will spare you the details, and once as I looked over the body of a young woman who had been killed in a head on collision. She probably perished instantly and never had any idea as to what had happened. Her arm caught my attention. An open wound on her shoulder exposed the yellow, fatty tissue, but the impact had killed her so quickly that the wound was left clean and bloodless, her heart never having pumped another drop. I stared into the wound, entranced by the dry bone beneath. The familiar feeling of narrowing vision and nausea overtook me and, now well experienced with my weak stomach, removed myself from the scene to the back of the air-conditioned chief's car to regain my composure.

Thinking that I was bothered by the incident, he came to check on me and wanted to know if I needed stress debriefing. However, the thing that bothered me wasn't the call at all, but the uncertainty about my ability to do the job, and I told him as much. He assured me that most of us had felt like that at one time or another, and that it would resolve as I gained experience and became more hands on. "You don't think about those things when your hands are busy," he explained. He was right. It faded in time, and I stopped viewing broken people as people and began to view them as a job to do. It was much easier if I didn't have time to think about it.

For many years of my career, I felt like the new guy, even as I shed rookie status and became rich in experience. Even now, there are some days that I still feel like I am feeling my way in the dark, and that has kept things exciting and new and my hands and head in the game. I have now overtaken most of my colleagues in years on the job. At the ripe old age of thirty-six, I am now the dependable old guy. Outside of the fire service, paramedics don't tend to stick around as long as they used to. Finding an old street medic is as rare as finding an elderly heroin junkie. Sure, they're around, but sooner or later, their life choices tend to wash them out, destroy their bodies, or they wise up and those not fortunate enough to move up, move on.

The twenty-year veteran of the street is truly a unicorn. I had those guys that I looked up to and never thought that I would become them. At some point, I crossed that bridge and never even noticed. With those years comes a lot of fatigue and the dreaded B word that inevitably comes for us all in this field, burnout. The first time I encountered the Z Dogg MD video that I referenced at the beginning of this book, it didn't resonate with me quite like it did the second time I watched it years later.

Everyone thinks it's the trauma of the calls that drives people from the field, and while there is an element of that, there is so much more to burnout. As this book progresses, I think you'll see how burnout occurs over the career cycle of a paramedic. I also hope that this book will provide a valuable inside look into the world of paramedicine and all the joy, heartache, headache, frustration, exhaustion, ups, downs, highlights, and lowlights that go with it.

I caution you that I have chronicled many of my experiences in detail and have left little to the imagination, so if you are squeamish, this may not be the read for you. However, I feel that those details are important to understanding my story and the relationships that we build with each other and with our patients. For the purposes of patient privacy, I have omitted or changed patient names, ages, locations, and other potential identifying factors. However, the crews that I have mentioned by name are real. They are my family and are as much a part of my story as my own wife and children.

CHAPTER 1

SLEEPLESS NIGHTS AND
BREAKING MINDS

It was the summer of 2019, and I sat in the back of an ambulance across from an agitated, mentally disturbed, homeless man whom a passerby had called in due to his strange behavior. We'll call him Leo.

We arrived to find a grizzly looking bearded man with deep creases in his forehead, a flannel shirt, dirty blue jeans, and mud caked sneakers separating at the soles. He reeked of last night's alcohol and stale urine. He was something of an urban evangelist for the church of who knows what and established his pulpit atop a concrete median in the middle of the road, yelling at passing cars as he stumbled in and out of traffic. His wrist was adorned with a faded hospital ID bracelet, and he carried a plastic grocery bag filled with various odds and ends. Among these items was a crumpled discharge summary from his last hospital visit (dated yesterday), a half-consumed bottle of water, an empty glass liquor bottle, a dead smartphone with a shattered screen, a half-smoked box of Newports—where he kept his $1.34 "that I had better not steal"—and a dirty pair of corduroys. These were likely all the possessions he owned in the world.

As I pulled up in the ambulance with flashing lights, he ignored me and continued with his tirade, directing his ire toward the air or some invisible entity that was clearly getting under his skin. Pacing as briskly as the alcohol would allow, he paused every few steps to regain his balance and used the opportunity to wave his arms and yell something before continuing his journey. I called out to him, but he turned his back to me, waved me off, and muttered something under his breath, clearly not wanting to deal with this yet again. I jogged down to confront him and cut off his path.

"How are you doing, sir? Is there something I can help with?" I asked.

He looked confused, and then angry. "Leave me alone, man."

He lifted his heavy foot to try to get around me. I stepped into his path again. "You seem upset. Why don't you step up here in the ambulance with me and we can talk about it."

"I can't find mah brother. I needa find mah brother!" he slurred, becoming more agitated by my encroachment.

"I'll tell you what, you step up in the truck with me and I'll take you to the hospital. We'll get you some dinner, a bed, and we'll see what we can do to find your brother," I reassured him.

His face softened, and his rigid brow relaxed, revealing the hollow sadness of a broken man in his eyes. He hesitated for a moment. "Yeah, alright." The hard part was done.

As we bumped down the road, I half-listened to his ramblings, since not much of it made sense anyway. Occasionally I asked him a pertinent question in an attempt to break his rambling loop and redirect him down a different thought path, but we always ended up right back in his rant. Occasionally, I nodded with an affirming "Mhm," but after three or four laps around that track, he called me out.

"You think I'm crazy!"

"No, sir. I just have to get this report done," I lied.

Satisfied with my answer, he continued with his story ad nauseum until the ambulance came to a halt and mid-sentence, I hopped up and directed him out the side door. Puzzled, and perhaps irritated by my interruption, he gave me a dirty look and questioned, "Where?"

"At the hospital," I explained again. "Remember? We gotta find your brother."

Now he was intrigued. "How the fuck you know 'bout mah brother?" he said, forgetting that he had just spent ten minutes telling me the incoherent story.

"C'mon, Leo. We'll sort all that out," I reassured him.

Reluctant, but now invested, he gathered his things and stepped out with me. The nurse stepped into the room casually with a, "What's going on?" I didn't want to talk in front of him, fearing that if I told her the truth in his presence, I might exacerbate his presently calm demeanor, so I pushed her back out to give her the rundown. She nodded and put on her psych hat. With my job done, I got her to sign for the package, and I departed.

I asked myself the question I am certain we all ask ourselves when we encounter a crazy person, How did he get like this? What was the event that finally made him snap? Hardly anyone is born crazy. Everyone has a story and, generally, it is not a single event that leads them to their destination, but a series of events that exposes the cracks. Just as water floods into the crevices in the road and expands them over time, creating potholes and craters with each deep freeze, so too, does repetitive stress, particularly when not dealt with in a healthy manner.

These days, many folks fill those holes with alcohol and heroin, which, as I'm sure you can deduce, is anything but healthy. There are, of course, medical and psychological reasons for the mind to break, but that's a book for someone to speak on who is more qualified than some dumb paramedic. In fact, this is not a medical or psychological examination at all. This book is a memoir, and it is how I choose to deal with those stresses. It's a collection of stories I wanted to commit to paper because, in general, folks are ignorant to the world I dwell in.

Along the way, some of my memories tend to indict the systemic failures that are leading to the exodus of workers from public service, high suicide rates, rising depression, poor job satisfaction, disproportionate divorce rates, and overall unhappiness among those who serve. This book should call into question the managerial practices, public assumptions, and deeply ingrained traditions that are causing this epidemic of negative outcomes and overall hopelessness among those who partake.

I tell the story of the homeless man because I see a correlation to the comedy of errors and tragedy of failures that have likely led that man to his present state of mind and the problems of public service and healthcare as a whole. I feel his plight, and I fear if we don't see changes in EMS soon, there will be a lot of us that become some version of him down the line.

Everyone in this field for any significant period of time is destined to feel the weight of burnout at some point. The smart ones bail before it consumes them, but some stay well past their expiration dates and absorb the check while unloading the weight of their negativity on everyone else. We all have a name to assign to that description, and I don't want to be that guy. I received advice early in my career I ignored at the time because it just seemed so damned unlikely, but lately, it permeates my thoughts more and more frequently. "When you don't love it anymore, it's time to go."

For a while, I have been feeling called to hang up my stethoscope and pursue a new path. To this point, it's been an amazing and rewarding experience, despite the bad days. I have enjoyed the respect the star of life on my chest garners and the way people clear away when I arrive, comfortable in the knowledge I will know what to do. I appreciate the appreciative families that have thanked me when I delivered their loved one back better than I found them and the camaraderie of the brotherhood into which I have been inducted. But more than anything, I have pride in the praises of my coworkers. "Man, you guys got hammered last night. Did you get any sleep?"

"Nope," I reply with disgust, but I am secretly proud that another shift is complete, and I have managed to get through an obscene number of calls without screwing anything up too badly. I wear that fifteenth call in twenty-four hours as a badge of honor.

This morning I was angry. I was ready to go home and put this day in the books. It was 6:15 AM, and I awoke to the sound of the bell going off. I had just laid down for the first time at 5:30 AM and had hoped to get an hour of sleep before the forty-minute drive home. I pounded my fist into my pillow but was surprised to hear that it was the ladder being called out to assist a person who had fallen out of bed. My frustration turned to elation at the realization that it wasn't for me— thank God.

Nonetheless, it was time to get up, and I packed my barely warmed bed away and sat impatiently waiting for my relief to arrive. I glanced at the clock; it was 6:29. We change shifts at 7:00 AM, and I expected my relief to come walking in at any moment. *He's probably sitting in the parking lot*, I thought to myself. I had made it, or so I believed, but I was shortsighted.

For the second time this morning, the bell went off, and this time, my unit number was called. I groaned in a mix of sheer exhaustion and frustration. Call number sixteen had just been dropped in my lap. The ladder call had turned out to be a bit more than just a person needing help up off the floor. I arrived to find a little old lady, who, according to them, just didn't look good. However, she didn't want to go, and they wanted me to check her out. I refrained from rolling my eyes and marched up the stairs with every intention of getting her to sign a refusal so I could get out of there. I glanced at my watch again, 6:40. I should have already been heading home.

As I walked into the room, I realized they were right. She really didn't look good. She was pale and sweaty, the kind of sweaty that means bad things.

You're not supposed to sweat when you're not hot, and if you are, it means there is a problem. I asked for a blood pressure cuff and a ladder guy stepped forward with one. I took it from him, and he was surprised. "Oh, *you're* gonna' do it?" he asked, as if he had never seen such things. It was low. Really low.

I doubled down on the advice of the ladder crew and reiterated the need for transport to the hospital, but she was still not having it. "Well let's sit you up and see how you feel," I proposed, not giving away my secret. Obliging my request, she raised to the edge of the bed, and just as I expected, immediately passed out. Now I could do what I needed to do. I caught her, and one of the ladder guys grabbed her legs, and we carried her to the stairs.

As she regained consciousness, she began to protest, but we ignored her. As far as we were concerned, she had to go. We were operating on the "implied consent" clause, an assumption that when unconscious, a reasonable person would want a paramedic to act in their best interest, and a trip to the hospital was in her best interest, whether she liked it or not. She could revoke it, but only while conscious, which she didn't remain for long. We placed her in her stair lift and in the middle of her protest, she passed out again. Implied consent returned, and we continued down the stairs.

As we got out to the truck, I was met with some unexpected praise. "You're bad ass, man. Ain't too many medics that will jump in there like that."

I smiled and jumped in the back of the ambulance, the door slamming behind me. "Let's go!" I yelled to the driver as he stepped into the back to assist me.

"You don't need anything?" he asked, confused. Nope. It was 6:50. Ten minutes until off time. I started IVs and did EKGs, hung IV fluids to raise her blood pressure, and checked her blood sugar. I started the assessment process over again, and we departed. At 7:03, I turned her over to the nurse and pushed my partner along to finish cleaning the ambulance. Sitting in the front seat, I feverishly typed out my narrative. It was time to go home, and I was not wasting any more time when we got back to the station.

When I arrived, my crew was gone. I was the last one there. I spoke a few words to the oncoming ambulance crew, wished them a good shift, and rushed out the door. I checked my watch again. 7:25. I had made good time. It hadn't even been an hour. I thought nothing more of it until three days later as we sat around the kitchen table.

During our morning meeting, we are each given the opportunity to relay anything important to the rest of the shift. Usually we tap the table in order, the signal to pass it to the next guy, and roll call is over. However, on this morning, as we completed the familiar cycle, tap, tap, tap, it stopped on the ladder officer from the morning of the previous shift. He didn't tap, and we all looked up as the rhythm was broken. He had something to say.

He retold the story of the little old lady and praised my actions. "I just want to say that I know you're taking it in the teeth out there, and you're tired and burnt out, but I am so impressed with the way that you handled that situation. It was shift change and a lot of medics would have had her sign the form and called it a day, but you still did the right thing, and I think that really says a lot about you. It seems that no matter how you're feeling, it never seems to affect your patient care and bedside manner."

I wore the compliment with pride, attempting to keep my smile to a goofy minimum. Those are the moments that keep me going. Those moments make an often difficult job, bearable. However, my attitude has changed a lot lately, and those good moments don't carry the weight they used to. I'm tired of the missed holidays, kid's baseball games and orchestra concerts, and the endless supply of everchanging antidepressants in hopes of finding one that doesn't make me a zombie, cause weight gain, and will still allow me to fulfill my duties in the middle of the night while being able to sleep when I am not at work.

I'm tired, and while my time on the street may be winding down, the love I once had for it will be eulogized on the pages of this book so that one day, after all is said and done, I can look back on the legacy left in the folks I have helped, the providers I have trained, the friendships I have built, and the good *and* bad days I was a part of. It's time to go though, so at the conclusion of this book, I am taking steps to leave the street to the next generation.

Chapter 2

The Men (And Women) Who Built Me

Let me introduce you to the characters of my story. These men and women are not the main characters, but in a sense, they are. You will meet many of them in the stories, but more importantly, I hope that you will see a little bit of each of them in me. I entered this field green, naïve, and completely ignorant of the world I was joining. These people adopted, molded, shaped, and polished me. They set expectations and challenged me to meet them, and when I met them, they raised the bar because they knew I was capable of more. For them, good was not good enough because they were great, and their expectation was that I would be great as well. They made me who I am. Each of them contributed something to the finished product.

You will also meet another type of character in this chapter. To a lesser degree, these characters shaped me as well. These are the characters that set the floor. If the sky was the limit for the first type of character, these folks were the ones that showed me what I did not want to be. I will not mention them by name. They will be given a pseudonym because my goal is not to shame them. In a sense, I feel sorry for them because they do not have the respect of their peers. They became what I feared, but they played an important part in my development as well, so their stories are worth telling.

Captain Boz

Boz is a recurring character in my story. A self-proclaimed reformed "hoodlum" out of the South Norfolk neighborhood in Chesapeake, Virginia, Boz entered the fire service in the mid-nineties. It has always been a role model job, but not necessarily the prestigious role model type job it is now. This was a time when "men's men" paved the way for the rest of us on meager salaries that did not sustain their families. Most shied away from a career, that paid barely above minimum wage, in which the expectation was that you would risk it all daily.

Self-contained breathing apparatus (SCBA) was still a new thing at that time, and there was a stigma around those who chose to wear it. You were a "pussy" if you wore "that shit." In retrospect, there are not many of those guys around anymore because of the now known risk of cancer caused by the smoke they inhaled. In any event, it took a special type of person to accept these conditions, and that type was wild and daredevilish with feelings of invincibility. When I paint that picture, that sounds a lot like the young Boz from the tales he told.

His younger days were filled with stories of a checkered history laced with drinking, bar brawls, getting one over on the cops, and chasing women before waking up and heading out for long blue collared days pulling wire on construction sites, and doing it all over again the next day.

When I met Boz in 2007, he was none of these things. He was introspective, collected, calculated, informed, and commanding. He was a father and a husband. I think there was something about raising a son that carried his name and a marriage to a good woman that tamed that wild spirit. However, even now, the spirit of defiance courses through his veins, but he channels it to more positive application these days.

He swore off alcohol, at least in front of his son, and made the conscious decision that because he had little self-control when drinking to excess, he stopped. For Boz, it was time to turn over a new leaf in pursuit of being a better man. His bar brawling days were over, but he was always prepared to throw down in a chief's office in defense of his men, a theme you will see play out in the stories to come. His drinking buddies grew up too and became the very cops they once eluded.

For Boz, the rules have always been more of a friendly suggestion, believing that a strong moral and ethical compass guides one to the right answer more often than a binder full of rules. He toed a fine line between being an effective company officer who supports the mission and vision of the chief who employs him, and presenting an effective argument to make the chief reconsider everything he believes. He's something of a street lawyer, and it was not uncommon for those who outranked him to leave his office boiling mad, knowing he was right, and left with the untenable position of sticking to their now debunked decisions or changing their position and looking weak. Most often, they chose obstinance.

For Boz, he lives by a simple code of ethics that does not need a manual. He had three rules. The first was four simple words. "Do what is right." Over the years, he imparted that wisdom upon me in several sticky circumstances where I had little confidence in my decisions. I would consult him for reassurance, and he would always turn it back on me. "Did you do what you thought was right?" After a moment of thought, my answer was always yes, to which his follow up response was, "Then you're fine. You can always defend doing what you thought was right, regardless of what the policy says." He didn't just expect it of us. He lived and breathed it, and I think that will be plain in the stories to come, so I don't need to elaborate on it here.

The second rule. "No Horseplay." He didn't want to defend it. He didn't want to answer for it. He didn't want anything to do with it. He told us if we were ever hurt in the station, he would put whatever we told him on the workman's compensation form, but he would not lie for us. For him, it went back to rule number one.

Rule three. "Know your job and be ready to do it when the tone goes off." These rules are so all encompassing that he didn't need any others. One night after the tone went off for the report of a structure fire, his lieutenant stopped to pee before going to the truck. For Boz, there was no greater sin. He was seething mad and lamented the fact someone would stop to relieve himself in someone's moment of greatest need, when everything they owned and had worked for was going up in flames and they needed a fireman. "Listen here, mother fucker. When that tone goes off, you get your ass to the truck. If you need a bathroom, I'll find you one when you get there, but you get your ass on that truck and piss your pants if you have to." For the next month, Boz woke that lieutenant up every two hours to go to the bathroom. There was no more waiting after that.

The only other time I ever saw Boz truly angry was on a late-night run in the pouring rain. We were clearing the call and I needed to back the engine up, and Boz found himself standing behind the engine as my lone spotter, getting soaked to the bone. In the meantime, the rookie, just a few days out of the academy, climbed up into the backseat and put his seatbelt on. This was not just a cardinal sin for Boz, but for firefighters in general. You never let the captain do what you could be doing, especially in the rain, and definitely not as the rookie.

I looked into the mirror to see Boz holding up his arms in the shape of an X, the signal to stop the truck. He disappeared around the back of the engine before the back door flew open. "Hey, mother fucker. I'm doing your damn job. Get your ass out here!" Boz then climbed into the captain's seat next to me and didn't say another word until we got back to the station. The rookie quit less than a week later, not because of this incident, but because he simply wasn't hacking it and we weren't letting him coast.

If you can't thrive under the leadership of Boz, you can't thrive anywhere. That was it. Some captains hold station detail cleaning days, expect rigorous adherence to policy, and hold station training on hydraulic calculations for pump pressures. Boz wanted you to do what was right with the promise to have your back if you could defend your position, refrain from horse play, and know your job and do it well. Anything else was secondary.

Without a micromanaging helicopter captain, I excelled under his leadership. I might be biased, but I think Boz fielded the best, most badass, engine company in the city, and he often did it with guys other officers dismissed as untouchable. When those officers couldn't correct the behavior they deemed intolerable, the so-called troublemaker got sent to Boz, and somehow Boz turned those behaviors into an asset and made us the most cohesive group around.

Aside from being a great leader, Boz served as an intergenerational historian and storyteller. He linked us to the past through stories of Captain Tackett and Ed Mizell, men who came ahead of him and taught and fostered him in the way he fostered us. For him, the stories were timeless, and he would often start with, "Do you remember when Tackett…," a man who had retired a decade before I even considered the fire service. There was no way I could have known Tackett, but somehow, Boz had a way of making me a part of the story, and I felt as if I did know the man because of the vibrant way in which Boz retold the tale for the dozenth time.

In this way, the new generation remembers and learns from the old and the traditions of the fire service persist. Boz carried that baton with the best of them. Through nine years under his leadership, my relationship with Boz developed from supervisor to coworker to friend and finally to father figure. He is the only one on this list I still talk to on a regular basis and still impacts my life to this day. To me, he is a giant.

Lieutenant Lackadaisical

Lieutenant Lackadaisical is the first of the "what not to be" influences, and as such, has been given a pseudonym. He was out of shape, a problem that he managed with a different fad diet every week. One week it was Atkins, the next a juice diet, and then perhaps the next, it would be the Subway diet, but none of them were effective because he was incapable of sticking with one. He was always looking to get one over on someone else. It didn't matter how unethical or out of bounds it seemed; if it was to his benefit, he was down for it. He was the kind of guy that got rules named after him.

At one point, he abused the trade policy and took a contract position in Iraq while simultaneously maintaining his employment with our department for an entire year. He was being paid so much on contract he could pay people to work for him in his position for less than his salary. He was making money from our department and on contract, and he wasn't even present in the US. Effectively, he was subcontracting his job so he could make higher salary elsewhere, but they couldn't terminate him because the chief had signed off on it. I have to believe that this was such a crazy ask that the chief did not understand the scope of what was being asked of him.

From day one, his lessons felt more like belittling than teaching. His goal seemed to be to make me feel insecure. "What are you good at?" was his first question to me. New to the department, I struggled with that answer. I didn't want to seem cocky, but I also didn't want to appear to lack confidence.

After a moment's thought, I responded, "Critical thinking." Instantly he hated that answer and used it as a club to beat me down.

"How does that translate to putting out fire?" he asked. "Did you critically think that tool into working?" He plugged my answer in wherever he could in ways that didn't make sense. I was irritated each time he brought it up, but I couldn't say anything. I was the rookie. Immediately, he established himself as an enemy and not an ally. I was not very receptive to his "wisdom" and critiques and avoided him whenever possible. Nevertheless, he outranked me, and he'd been around for a long time, so I did my best to show the proper reverence. There were definitely some things I could learn from him.

On one occasion, we had had a fire and I was enthusiastic about getting to be the nozzleman for the first time. When we got back to the station, he took the wind out of my sails when he asked, "What color was the house?" I had no idea. "You didn't look?" he pressed. I had to admit I hadn't. It was on fire, why would I care about the color of the house? "You should always look at the house before you go in. Look to see if there are toys in the yard that might indicate there are kids inside. Is the hood of the car warm? It might tell you if the occupant is at home. Is there smoke coming from the eaves or below the house? It might tell you that there is fire over your head or under your feet. Always look at the house." I learned a valuable lesson about scene awareness I carry with me even now.

Months later, I was dispatched to another fire directly behind the station. I got dressed prior to getting on the truck, but he was slow and threw his gear on the truck, telling the driver to go. "I will get dressed when we get there," he said.

As we arrived, there was smoke pushing out through the front door. I pulled the hose line and stacked up at the front door to pull my mask onto my face. I was ready. Looking back, I saw him lazily walking up to the door while pulling his arm into the sleeve of his coat. He attempted to close it, but the zipper was broken, and the Velcro worn out. It wouldn't close. He shook his head in disbelief. "Just go in," he told me. I knew better. I had been taught "two in, two out." You never go in by yourself, but he was a ranking officer, and I was not in any position to question his order.

I advanced the hose line into the darkness and listened for the roar of the fire. I heard it in front of me. Crawling forward on my knees, I was suddenly aware of a rapid rise in temperature. It was hotter than any fire I had experienced previously, and I hadn't even found it yet. *Man, my neck is burning,* I thought. I paused for a moment to think. Looking up, I saw the ceiling ignite and flames push toward the door behind me. With the door now open, the fire had found a desperately needed air source and was stretching its tendrils to reach it. From the corner of my eye, I noticed an orange flash, and then a second, and a third.

Looking around, I didn't see any fire except what was above my head, but then I made a connection. I had learned about this fire behavior in school. This is a condition known as rollover, where the superheated gas at the ceiling level has found enough air to ignite. The next stage is flashover. Flashover is the point in which everything in the room has enough air, fuel, and heat to spontaneously ignite at once. The flashing I was seeing around me was literally the smoke igniting inches from my face. It had the heat, and it had the fuel. All it needed was the air and behind me, the open door was threatening to supply it.

Realizing I was in trouble, and with the rising temperature in the room becoming unbearable, the fight or flight instinct raged inside me, and my panicked body implored me to retreat. On the other side of the coin, I was still new to this. *Maybe this is just how it is sometimes. Maybe it's not as bad it seems*, I thought. I did not want to be thought a coward and seen running out the door from a fire. Panic and reason wrestled for control of my body, and I fought the urge to run. *Keep your head. Don't panic, breathe slower, you know what to do*, my inner monologue coached me.

I did know what to do. I recalled an academy lesson where I was taught to widen the hose stream to a fog cone pattern and aim it at the ceiling to establish a protective cooling cone around my body if ever I found myself in an impending flashover. My mind flashed back to the lesson. "In the old days, we didn't put water on smoke, but now they call smoke 'black fire,' aptly named for its ability to burn you without the presence of visible flames. Cool it down if it gets too hot," I could hear Chief Fly saying.

Falling back on that training, I did just that and saw the ceiling darken, and the flashes around me grew dim. The room cooled immediately. I could now see the dull orange glow in front of me and pushed forward until I found it roaring above my head. I opened the nozzle once more, and the room darkened again. At last, I felt Lt. Lackadaisical tap me on the shoulder. "Are you good?" he asked. "Where's the fire?"

"I put it out," I told him.

"Good. Let's back out and regroup."

Later at the station, I told him about the rollover and the near flashover. He was unimpressed. "What color was the house?" he asked again. This time, I was prepared.

"Yellow, with bricks on the front," I answered, walking out of the room.

I was disgusted that he had the nerve to attempt a "gotcha" when he was not even prepared to be by my side. He hadn't checked his gear. He hadn't gotten dressed. He was slow to the truck, and he left me alone in an extremely dangerous situation . His lack of preparation could have gotten me killed, and yet here he was acting like I was the one that needed the lesson. I remembered another lesson they drilled into us in school. "Complacency kills." I now understood what they meant. Do as I say, not as I do, I suppose. I made a mental note, *Never be like that guy.*

Lieutenant BJ

BJ was an opportunity that I pissed away. He was a brand-new officer when I met him in 2007 but had been given charge of a ladder truck soon after promotion. This was relatively unheard of, as the position of Ladder Lieutenant was coveted and usually given to senior lieutenants with years of experience. The truck itself was typically staffed with senior firefighters who could operate without much direction. The ladder truck is filled with equipment requiring a vast amount of technical knowledge, and crew members are expected to operate in zero visibility, high hazard environments without the protection of a hose line.

Remember my lesson about cooling the room? That option wouldn't have been available to a ladder guy, so you had better know what you were doing. Giving this position to a junior officer expressed supreme confidence in his abilities. It was well placed. He was cerebral, personable, and the physical image of what a firefighter should be. He was a good fit for the position. What he did not expect was to be given a scrawny, arrogant kid, fresh out of the academy, to lead.

On most days, his senior man had five years of experience. That meant he, with eight years on the job, had three more years than both of us combined. BJ accepted the challenge. He spent his days quizzing me about policy, placing him in stark contrast to Boz. His favorite policy pertained to acceptable carbon monoxide levels and where the poisonous gas could be most effectively ventilated. He attempted to train me on tools that we would never use and placed particular emphasis on physical fitness.

I did not mesh well with BJ, not because of him, but because I did not know what I did not know. He was trying to impress upon me the need to be "combat ready," not for the everyday run of the mill call, but for the obscure call when people were relying on me and there wasn't time to figure out how to work the airbags or rapid intervention air pack, which would be deployed when a firefighter was down in a fire.

To me, I was fresh out of the academy, in peak shape, and I already knew it all. BJ was too early for me. While he tried to develop me as a firefighter, I needed development as a person. I resisted every step of the way while BJ tried everything he could think of. He made workouts mandatory on his crew while I faked injuries to get out of them. He questioned me in front of people hoping that I would be shamed into conforming, but I was shameless. He set up training drills, and I did them reluctantly while complaining the whole time. In the end, I transferred to the engine under Boz.

The fact was, I hated ladder work and had a much greater affinity for EMS, which I could get on the engine. In addition, I wasn't forced to work out anymore. Boz's leadership style was a better fit for the personal development I still required. Even still, just across the bay, I was still in the sphere of BJ's influence, and even if he couldn't make me work out, he could still train me, and I would still occasionally be on his truck.

It is because of him I know that carbon monoxide levels under nine parts per million are acceptable for residential buildings and under fifty ppm is acceptable for commercial buildings, and that the poisonous gas is lighter than air, and therefore best ventilated from the top of the window. It wasn't until eight years later I would fully grasp what it meant to be combat ready and understand the importance of the lessons BJ did his best to teach me.

I was asleep and awakened to the blaring tones screaming at me from the speaker above my bed. "Residential structure fire. Engine 10 Respond." Firefighters move faster for fire than we do for EMS calls. This is what we all sign up for, so from the moment we hear those words, it's a race to pull on our pants and boots, jockeying for position as we stampede down the hall, slamming into the walls as we go. National Fire Protection Agency (NFPA) standards say we are to be "turned out," or in full protective gear, in sixty seconds or less from the time of dispatch. Most of us easily beat that, and on Engine 10, we took pride in beating others into their district. Others tried to beat us into ours but to my recollection, it never happened, and it wasn't going to tonight either.

The fire was across the street, and we could see the glow of the flames and black smoke pouring into the sky from the apron of the fire station. Boz called a working fire before we even pulled out the door. We would be on scene almost before I could buckle my seatbelt.

From the outset, this was a defensive fire. The house was too far gone to risk firefighter safety, and Boz directed me to pull an inch and a half line to protect exposures. I pulled the line, donned my mask, and advanced the hose to the side of the house when Boz told me he had received a report of someone trapped inside. Our mission had changed. Just seconds before, Boz had told me this fire was too dangerous to go into, and now he was telling me to get ready because we were going in.

The flames ripped through the back door where we made entry. I opened the nozzle and the stream disappeared into the inferno, but its thirst was insatiable, and it pushed out toward me, lapping at my helmet. I ducked down and moved the nozzle in rapid circular motions, a technique for disrupting what is known as thermal layering. This disperses the heat from floor to ceiling and makes the fire easier to put out.

The fire began to die down, and I pushed in and killed the remaining glow in what we now knew to be the kitchen. In front of me, I heard a voice. "Found her! Give me a hand!" My best friend, Ryan, had found the victim. She lay just outside of the kitchen in a narrow hallway where Ryan had approached from the front door. He grabbed her feet, and I dropped the nozzle and grabbed her arms, and we moved toward the door. As we moved, I struggled to maintain my grip. Her skin sloughed off and wept. Combined with the moisture I had injected into the environment, the mixture rendered her extremities the texture of an eel, and I couldn't hold on. We paused three times in the twelve-foot walk to the door to readjust our grips. The battle with my hands in oversized wet gloves had exhausted me. At eighty pounds, this woman might as well have been an elephant because I had nothing left to give.

I had extinguished the fire and removed the victim, and I was happy to turn her over to someone else so I could catch my breath. I stopped at the porch, lowered her to the ground, and waited for relief, but Ryan was keen on seeing the job through. Still holding her legs, he continued down the steps, and she went with him. With me no longer holding her top half, her head slammed down each step before others recognized what was going on and screamed for us to stop.

The medics scooped her up, and she disappeared into the night in the back of their ambulance. I was embarrassed by my error, but at that moment, I couldn't think about anything else except my inability to breathe. I pulled my regulator off my face mask and was overtaken by the smell of burnt flesh. Peering down at my gloves, I saw the burnt skin of my victim melted to them. Nauseated, I ripped them off and threw them on the ground. This was more than my stomach could handle. My heart was pounding, and my body was moving blood away from my extremities and non-essential organs in favor of supplying my brain, heart, and lungs. I felt lightheaded and heaved the contents of my stomach into the bushes.

Boz emerged from the structure. "Are you ready to go back in?" he asked. I was not. I felt awful. "Go sit down, and I'll pull someone else," he directed me. I obliged. While watching others do the job I should have been doing, BJ's lessons had suddenly become clear. I had done a piss poor job of rescuing a tiny elderly woman. My body had not held up to six or seven minutes of high intensity work. I was not combat ready. What if it had been one of my brothers? I am confident I would not have been able to rescue them. At year eight, for the first time, I was humbled and left with a thought. *Is this the career that I really wanted to do for the rest of my life? Was I just collecting a paycheck?*

Chris

Best known for his no nonsense approach to patient care, I credit Chris with my transition from middle-class, suburban, white boy to gritty hood medic. Leave your bullshit at the door, Chris didn't want to hear it. In retrospect, I think Chris was long past burnout, but he wore it in such a way that worked in the environment he was in. Chris is the first of the four highly skilled medics I was blessed to be surrounded by as I learned my trade.

If you are sick or injured, he is the man you want. He cuts through the fluff and gets to the problem, fixes it, and gets rid of you. If you aren't really sick, you don't want to see Chris show up. It's going to be a long, uncomfortable ride to the hospital for you. To say Chris didn't care would be a fallacy, but he really was not fazed by much of anything. I once watched him walk up to a patient's house with a cup of coffee in one hand and an iPad in his other. It is this kind of nonchalant attitude that really made me admire Chris.

When I went to a call as a new medic, I was running protocols through my mind, considering worst case scenarios, and making "if this, then that" decisions preemptively. When Chris responded to a call, he was playing a game on his iPad. Once, when I asked him what the call was, he didn't even look up. Focused on his game, he just said, "Fuck if I know. Some bullshit, probably." And he was right. It doesn't matter because it's the same every time. The dispatch notes are always inaccurate and based on the very poor health knowledge of the average person. It's never what they say it is, so you might as well find out when you get there.

Chris has one mode; let's go. He doesn't need to talk to you to decide "sick or not sick." He just needs to look at you. Pulling up to the scene, he was already pulling his seatbelt off and opening the door as I stopped. "Don't even get out," he would sometimes say as he bailed from the barely stopped truck. "Let's go," he'd tell the patient. The rest could be done in transit.

If he had to walk into your residence, and he decided you weren't sick, his first question was simple. "Do you want to go to the hospital?" You had better not hesitate because the bus was leaving. If yes, then his next words were, "Then let's go." Already turning to leave.

Sometimes the patients would protest. "I can't walk, my stomach hurts!"

Chris would reply, "Your legs ain't broke. Let's go." If you were sick, it was *really* "go" time for Chris. He was already three steps ahead of everyone else. Once, we arrived to an asthmatic who drew his final breath in front of us before "circling the drain," as we say, and passing out. He collapsed, and Chris didn't need to assess him any further to know what was going on. He immediately started barking orders. "I need a BVM (Bag valve mask for providing breaths to the patient), epi, set up a mag drip and an inline neb kit, and let's go!" he said while dragging the man twice his size onto the stretcher. By the time we arrived at the hospital, the man was awake and talking. A moment's hesitation and the outcome would have been different. Chris was the man for the job in the moment.

His innate ability to understand what was wrong by sight alone and cut through the shit was something I envied and a skill I set my sights on obtaining from the very beginning. I quickly learned that skill is not learnable. It's instinct, and you either have it or you don't. You can refine the instinct, however, with experience. Even while I was uncertain, I think Chris saw I had it, and he was one of my biggest supporters to further my education. "You'd make a good medic," he'd tell me. It was the highest form of compliment from someone I so respected, but from all outward appearances, seemed unpleasable.

It wasn't that he was unpleasable. He was just jaded from years on the street, and the attitude guarded a huge teddy bear heart a lucky few get to be a part of. He held himself to seemingly impossible standards and expected the same level of patient care from those around him. He had very little tolerance for bullshit, and if he deemed you not worth his time, then he wasn't going to waste it on you.

By all accounts, from those who know him, Chris was one of the best medics around, and students were frequently paired with him. If you watch closely, you're going to learn a lot in a day with Chris, but you had better come with the basic knowledge and skillset expected of a paramedic student.

Once, a middle-aged student was assigned to Chris for the day. He had grown bored in his nine to five career and decided to make a change to something more exciting. EMS is the natural place that a lot of these folks find themselves for act two. In his final semester, the student should have been proficient in most skills and nearly able to function by himself as a paramedic, and that is what Chris expected of him.

We were dispatched to a critical call for another patient "circling the drain," and after waiting for the student to take charge and failing to do so, Chris took over and asked the student to set up a dopamine drip. The student stared back at him blankly. "Never mind. Take this and bag the patient, and I'll do it.," Chris said, handing the student a BVM. The student took the device, and then proceeded to look at it, turning it over and over in his hands. Chris looked back after several seconds to find him still not doing what was asked of him. "What's the problem?" Chris demanded.

Timidly, the student said, "I don't know how to use this."

"Are you fucking serious? Get the fuck out of my ambulance. You're in my way!" he said, pushing him out of the way. "Take him back to the station," he told the engine officer.

After the call, Chris pulled him into a meeting and explained he could not be expected to teach him advanced skills if he was not even proficient at a basic level. He recommended the student stay an EMT for a while longer, run some calls, and gain some experience before proceeding further. "But I have to be honest, I'm not sure you're cut out for this career. You might want to take stock of your skills and abilities and decide if this is for you." And that was that. With a scathing review from his preceptor and being sent home mid-shift, the student was dropped from the program, thereby saving hundreds of lives.

By contrast, as I went through medic school, Chris would often disagree with my treatment plan, but he would say nothing because I was stepping up and taking charge. It wasn't that I was doing anything wrong. Usually it was a case of overtreating and making something ALS when it didn't need to be. Students do this out of fear of missing something and not knowing what they don't know. Chris had seen these things hundreds of times but knew that I had not, so he let me come to my own conclusions.

Later, he might make a recommendation for doing something differently or lightly rib me for starting an IV and giving pain medicine when it clearly wasn't justified. But that's how you learn, and the jokes were better than the disapproving looks from doctors who disagreed with my treatment. Though he was a little rough around the edges, that grit made me razor sharp, and I cannot imagine that I would have become the medic I am without Chris around in those early years.

B-Bock

If Chris was the yin, ol' B-Bock was the yang. After three decades in EMS, Bock had seen and done it all, but his approach to patient care was completely different than that of Chris. Equally as competent and just as much of a badass, he used words like "sweetie" with the elderly ladies and sat down to talk with them before making suggestions. He moved a bit slower and thought things through because *his* experience had taught him the story was in the details.

He was also exceedingly patient. As I completed my internship in pursuit of my EMT- Intermediate, I encountered a patient complaining of dizziness. After placing him on the monitor to get a look at his heart activity, I noticed he had a fast heartrate and a rhythm that looked to me like supraventricular tachycardia. This rhythm is considered a potentially lethal rhythm, and I instantly made the decision that the treatment was electricity. Ripping out the defibrillation pads and slapping them on his chest, I heard Bock calmly speak up behind me. "Whoa there, Chadley. What are you gonna do with those?"

"I'm going to cardiovert him," I stated confidently.

"You're going to shock sinus tach?" he asked, amused and peeling the pads away.

Sinus tachycardia is basically a normal heart rhythm that is just a little faster. If you are running, you're in sinus tach. By this point, the patient was looking back and forth between us, confused and more than a little nervous about the overzealous, young medic in charge of his care. "I think we'll hold off on that," Bock said, laughing.

I printed the strip, and there in the squiggly lines was the p wave, which indicated a normal heart rhythm. "He's just dehydrated," Bock explained. "Let's give him some fluids and see if his rate comes down." I was embarrassed by my rash reaction and suddenly realized I was not yet ready to handle things on my own.

Later at the station, I was downtrodden, and B-Bock asked what was wrong. "I would have shocked that guy," I explained. Bock leaned back in his chair and put his hands behind his head, smiling at me.

"You'll be alright, Chadley. You just need to slow down a little bit," he reassured me. And just like that, with a few simple words of affirmation, B-Bock restored my confidence while providing a valuable lesson. Bock was a big believer in "BLS before ALS" and was often hesitant to initiate advanced treatment before we had exhausted all basic treatment options. "Just because you can, doesn't mean you should," he'd say.

As I furthered my training, this was a lesson that took me awhile to learn, but eventually, I got it. Nonetheless, B-Bock never missed an opportunity to offer me the defibrillation pads and ask if I wanted to use them when sinus tach showed up on the monitor.

Miss Amy

Miss Amy was a glue-like force in the station. The only one on this list considered a "civilian paramedic," she was no less one of the guys than anyone else and contributed immensely to group cohesiveness. She was the station mama and famous for her baked goods, most specifically the checkerboard cake, which was always a treat when it showed up.

Her and B-Bock were the OG's. They were part of Portsmouth EMS when it was still American Medical Response before the fire department took it over. They had stories of being stationed at Station 6, a nightmare station in terms of run volume, and transporting to Portsmouth General, both of which had long since faded into the fabric of Portsmouth history and disappeared from the landscape.

Mrs. Amy is another one I admire for her longevity and ability to remain the same medic I assume she was at the beginning of her career. She was sweet to a fault. Sometimes we would get a complaint so dumb I would sit back and wait for her wrath, but it never came. She treated it the same as the heart attacks and strokes and investigated it with the same degree of suspicion she would any of the more serious complaints.

In fact, that is what I most admired about Mrs. Amy. Her assessment never deviated. It was the same every time. In school, we are taught you follow the algorithm to pass the test but once you get to the street, you can essentially throw it out and find your own way of doing things…to a point. Mrs. Amy's assessment looked like the testing sheets used to grade the students. From the top of the head to the tip of the toes, everything was evaluated and as such, nothing was ever missed.

One of my favorite things about Mrs. Amy was her documentation. You could learn so much from what she documented, and I would often find she had noticed something I had not. In discussions with her, she would explain what that finding was indicative of and why she felt it important to write it down. To this day, I maintain her documentation style if for no other reason than it keeps me on task and from missing things, and I teach it to the students passing through who all leave with a better understanding of patient assessment and documentation.

Her legacy will live on long past my departure and in states far from her reach. Even with her sweet demeanor, you could never underestimate Mrs. Amy's propensity to become an absolute badass when the situation demanded it. I could elaborate here, but there is a fantastic story that you will read later that demonstrates this.

Tim Schatti

Tim was like the metaphorical duck on a pond. The fourth medic on this list I was blessed to learn from, his knowledge and experience was probably the most diverse of those I've mentioned. He had worked in EMS in a variety of facets, including with Virginia Beach EMS and in private ambulance capacities. He was a critical care paramedic and had a wide array of technical knowledge and abilities that went well beyond the typical scope of a normal paramedic, including ventilator and balloon pump management.

It wasn't Tim's KSAs that most impressed me though. It was his ability to never change his facial expression, no matter what he was dealing with. I cannot reiterate this enough. The demeanor of the person in charge sets the tone for how a call is going to go. There are times when it would be easy to let emotion dictate the tone, but for Tim, that just wasn't in his DNA.

Late one night, Tim was dispatched to the report of "bleeding." When he arrived, he was greeted by frantic parents carrying the limp body of their little girl before he could even open the ambulance door. Dad was covered in blood. A few days prior, she had had a tonsillectomy, and the sutures had ruptured, essentially drowning her in her own blood. Tim calmly took the child and called for an engine to assist.

I was on the response, and as I opened the door, I found Tim opening the package of an intubation tube. "What do you have?" I asked.

Without changing his facial expression, he simply said, "A cardiac arrest. Get me an IV please." And that's how that call went from start to finish. I am pleased to report the child survived and made a full recovery.

If Tim had a flaw, it's that he didn't wake up well. He had an uncanny ability to function without even knowing what he was doing. On more than one occasion, I watched him wake up in the middle of a call. His eyes had been open, and he had been going through the motions, but you could watch the life enter his eyes. As he looked around, he would ask "What were we here for?" None of us realized it though, because his "fully awake" and "fully asleep but functioning" demeanor were exactly the same.

Paramedic Shouldabeenfired

The lessons we learn from mistakes are far more impactful than the ones we learn from what we did right. Paramedic Shouldabeenfired was a walking mistake. We could also have called him Paramedic Nevershouldabeenhired.

He had decades of experience, but he was the kind of medic that we call a "Para-god." Para-gods don't need protocols, and oversight is an inconvenience. They have been doing this forever and, at some point, read a journal article "that said…," so they apply their knowledge and do whatever they want. It usually works out, until it doesn't.

He possessed the bedside manner of a porcupine and was by and large disliked for his arrogance within the station as well. To make matters worse, he was a militant atheist. Often, a patient would begin to pray, or say something like, "Oh, God. Help me!"

And he would reply, "God can't save you, but I can," or "You don't have to call me God, my name is…." It was disgusting.

I was partnered with him on the ambulance on one of my early shifts in the department, and we were dispatched to the report of a chest pain. As we arrived, Paramedic Shouldabeenfired spent forty-five minutes downplaying the patient's symptoms and attempting to talk him out of going to the hospital. When the patient's wife finally told him to just take him, he replied, "Well it's only three minutes away; you could just drive him."

At this point, the lady was seething. "Just put him in the ambulance and take him! I don't understand why this is such a big deal," she demanded.

He finally relented and walked the man to the ambulance.

A few weeks later, the patient's wife filed a complaint, and the EMS supervisor called me to get my side of the story. This put me in a serious bind. As the new guy, I did not want the reputation for ratting out a coworker, but the event had weighed heavily on me since it had happened. In my mind, there was no question that I would report the truth, but I had to seriously evaluate how much I would soften that truth. In the end, my moral compass won, and I confirmed her version of events to the letter.

He was given a three-day suspension, a slap on the wrist in my opinion. To be honest, I didn't learn much from this scenario. The "what not to do's" were so egregious that common sense told me that this was not the medic I wanted to be, but throughout my career, he has served as the frame of reference for bottom of the barrel. When I went through paramedic school, I continually told myself, *If that guy can do it, anybody can.*

These folks have impacted me heavily, and I have attempted to adopt their strengths. From Boz, I learned about effective leadership, how to be decisive, and was given confidence to worry less about the technicalities of the written rule and to follow my own moral compass. From BJ, I learned about combat readiness and being prepared for the worst-case scenario for when that day inevitably came. He gave me the understanding to honestly self-evaluate and to make a change when I realized I wasn't living up to the standard.

From Chris, I learned how to handle myself on the streets, how to know when it was "go time," and set high expectations of myself. He also gave me the latitude to make mistakes and to learn from them and the encouragement I needed to become better. From B-Bock, I learned how to slow down, the art of the bedside manner, and how to carry myself with grace amidst tragedy, which I will discuss in a later chapter.

Mrs. Amy taught me to be thorough and was the template for teaching others that I model myself after to this day. Schatti taught me that no matter how good you are, when you keep a level head and a calming demeanor, everyone around you is better and the call goes much more smoothly.

The fact is, none of these people exist in a vacuum. Each one of them exhibit elements of each one of these strengths, but the character traits that really made them stand out are traits I tried to adopt for myself so I could be the best paramedic possible. I hope I have made them proud.

Chapter 3

A History of Firsts

I have a history of firsts. My first of anything is *always* anything but ordinary or easy. With every new beginning, I have come to expect catastrophe, a baptism by fire that will test my limits. I have learned to approach each first day, first year, new certification, new job, etc. cautiously. I tell my new partners to expect the worst. They usually laugh me off, and then are flabbergasted when my predictions come true. "Well I'll be damned. You called it," they ruminate. Some medics are "black clouds," the term given to people who are absolute magnets for the proverbial fecal matter. Some are "white clouds," the term assigned to those who never seem to get anything interesting. Generally, my skies are clear. My black cloud only hangs over new beginnings, or perhaps I am just on higher alert on those days.

First Night on the Ambulance

My first night on an ambulance as a career Firefighter/EMT, I was baptized, not by an emergency, but a prank, or so I thought. I pulled into the hospital, turned over the patient with Mrs. Amy, remade the stretcher, and headed back out to attend to my duties of cleaning up the ambulance. I returned to the parking area to find the ambulance was not where I had left it. I considered all the possible scenarios.

Maybe I had come out the wrong entrance. I paced back and forth before deciding, no, I remembered those signs, that post, and that jagged piece of metal where so many ambulances had scraped their bumper. Maybe Mrs. Amy had moved it, but she hadn't come out of the hospital yet. She was still talking to the doctor, so that seemed unlikely. Then, a sudden realization hit me. I was the new guy. I had been warned of pranks and told to take them in stride, don't let them see you sweat, laugh it off, and clean up the mess. This had to be a firefighter playing a joke on me. Maybe Mrs. Amy was even in on it.

I really didn't want to give them the satisfaction, but I couldn't just sit there with my thumb up my butt and wait for the big reveal. I'd go in and give them their thrill, laugh it up with them, and get back to work. I found Mrs. Amy typing away at the EMS desk. "Uh, did you move the ambulance?" I asked timidly.

"No, why?" she replied, unphased by my question, and not looking up from her report.

"It's…um, it's gone." She stopped typing.

"What do you mean it's gone?"

"I went outside, and it's just…not there."

Not believing me, she stood up and walked outside with me in tow, struggling to keep up. I began to realize she was not in on it at all, and this wasn't just a prank. My heart sank, and my days old career flashed before my eyes. If I wasn't fired, I would now be known as the guy that got his ambulance stolen the first time he was entrusted with it.

We stepped outside, and to my surprise, there it was. Backing across the parking lot, slowly, was the ambulance with the steady, high-pitched beep of the backup alarm as it's soundtrack. "Hood" Amy had just possessed Mrs. Amy's body. She radioed for police, and I went to get security and sat back while Miss Amy handled her—er—*my* business.

I got a firsthand view of what it takes to be an urban city medic. Miss Amy was old school. She didn't take any crap, but she didn't give any either, as long as you treated her with respect. This guy had crossed her before he even knew she existed, and tonight, he was going to feel her wrath. She slammed the radio against the glass on the passenger side door. He was looking in the driver's side mirror, and she scared the absolute holy bajeezus out of him. The ambulance lurched backwards as it came to a sudden stop, and then rocked back and forth.

He knew that he'd been caught. He put it in park and opened the door with a smug grin. She wasn't smiling as she dragged him out by the arm, pinning him against the side of the ambulance, wrenching his arm behind his back. He wasn't smiling anymore either as he begged for mercy. I remained an observer, still uncertain as to what my role was here. Security arrived to take over the detainment, and then police to arrest him. He was drunk, and when asked why he took it, he said, "Well the keys were in it." Well then, by all means, don't let us get in your way. My career in EMS began with a stolen ambulance. Welcome to the show, kid.

First Structure Fire

My first fire was the stuff movies are made of. Three months into the job and it almost killed me and several others. I learned a new term that day, "smoke explosion," and I gained a front row seat to the unpredictability and danger of the job. There are articles written about our specific event because it is such a rare occurrence. So rare, in fact, that even when I describe it years later to veteran firefighters, they correct me and tell me what I experienced was a backdraft, but they're incorrect, and I pull up the articles to show them why.

I was on the ladder truck with Lieutenant BJ, and we were responding downtown to a church fire. As the radio crackled to life, it was clear this was going to be a big event. We could see the flames rising over the treetops from the interstate several miles away. When I arrived, I was disappointed to find I would not even be able to see the show, let alone participate in it. Our assignment was to park on the opposite side of the block, put up the stick (the slang term for the giant ladder on top of the truck), and flow water over the buildings into the back of the church building, which was now fully engulfed and threatening to take other structures with it. Lieutenant BJ, something of a muscle headed prophet, proved himself a genius when he directed the driver to park on the opposite side of the median, facing into oncoming traffic. "I don't want to be too close to this building, in case it catches fire," he explained.

The stick went up, the water began to flow, and I scurried up to direct the flow. Once in place, I slid back down and stood on the turn table. BJ was unhappy with the positioning and told me to go back up and move it around. I didn't understand the directions, went up, adjusted it, and again, scurried back down. By now, frustrated that his dumb rookie wasn't smart enough to figure this simple task out, he decided to do it himself. He made the 105-foot climb to the top and anchored in for the long haul as he had expected me to do, using his radio to direct ladder streams from the other trucks, who were now mired in a cloud of black smoke, to the point of the largest flames.

The church was a lost cause, and this was now a "surround and drown" operation of an entire city block. I stood on the turn table of the ladder truck, prepared to move the ladder around at his direction, and below me, three guys had stacked up at the door of the adjacent building to put on their SCBA, preparing to enter and check for fire extension. It was to be a quick assignment, a formality for the chief, a box to check on the report later to prove we had done our due diligence. They had already broken the lock and pried the doors open, and at the time, there was no evidence of any fire in that building. All was quiet, for now. *The property owner is going to be pissed that we broke their door for nothing*, I thought.

That's when it happened. A dull rumble shook the ground, getting louder with each passing second, followed by the crash of breaking glass. In front of me, one by one, straight down the row, the windows blew out of the side of the building. The roof rolled forward from back to front, lifting and then settling back onto the walls, like the crowd doing the wave at a baseball game. Then suddenly, the pressure in the air changed. The air in my lungs was sucked out and just as quickly forced back in, and then…*boom*!

I looked up to see the front of the building explode outward toward me. I turned my back to the flying debris and took airborne bricks to the back, protected by the helmet on my head and the air pack hanging from my shoulders. Then, just like that, it was over. There was no fire, no smoke, no nothing. All around me lay the rubble of the building, present only moments before, and now gone. The scene was reminiscent of documentaries about WWII and images of London and France after the Luftwaffe had dropped their ordinance on them. It was surreal.

The scene had gone still and quiet, pierced only by the sound of a motion detecting device screeching from an awestruck firefighter who had sat motionless for too long. But then, the radio came to life from units all over the fireground, stepping on each other and frantically trying to relay the incident from their perspective as if we had not all just experienced the same thing. Over the air came a calming voice, a voice of reason, the voice of the battalion chief in command. "All units hold your traffic for personnel accountability."

It suddenly occurred to me there had been guys standing where the pile of rubble now lay just moments before the explosion. Shit. I vacated my position atop the ladder turn table and ran to dig them out, but I soon found it was unnecessary. In a narrow clearing next to the building, I found them standing, completely free of the debris. The second story wall had fallen over them, missing them by inches. Had they been standing just three more feet away from the wall, they would have been crushed. But here they were, injured, but not seriously. Miraculously, nobody was killed.

BJ joined me on the ground. He took stock of his head, neck, chest, stomach, gonads, arms, and legs. All were present and accounted for. "What the hell?" he said. Now standing atop the debris pile, he looked down at the ground where the truck could have been sitting if he hadn't made the decision to change sides and then back at the truck. I nodded, an open acknowledgement of his lifesaving decision, as he reached over and pulled a brick out from between my shoulders and air pack.

Brand New Paramedic

And then there was my first night on my own as a newly ordained paramedic, fresh with the blessing of the medical director to go forth and do hero stuff. At this point, EMS definitely wasn't new to me anymore, but the proverbial monkey is heavier when it's on your back. As I sat at the hospital working on the report after the first call of my shift, I heard the tones of my station followed by an ambulance from another district dispatched. That would never do.

I've worked with dozens of medics over the years that are content to let others take their runs, but I was now in charge of this truck, and I was not going to develop that reputation. So I collected my computer and radioed to dispatch I would take it. "What is it?" my partner asked.

"Just a car accident," I said with the indifference of someone who had run hundreds of other fender benders that did not warrant an ambulance. The lights kicked on, the sirens wailed, and I ignored the radio while finishing my report. I never heard the key words that should have triggered some sense of urgency like "fatality" and "powerlines down." And so I arrived oblivious to the circumstances but quickly learned this wasn't just another fender bender.

There are things I don't remember. For instance, I don't remember stepping over a body with a missing leg lying in the street. I didn't notice the live power line hanging just above my head, and I have no idea how I wasn't electrocuted when I learned later it was just a few feet above me when I walked under it. I never saw the deceased victim bent backwards over the passenger seat of the car, which was folded in half and wrapped around the tree. They were not my patients. I was directed to take the kid sitting on the curb who was seemingly fine.

In the darkness, I ran through the qualifying questions. "Are you hurt?" No.

"Does this hurt?" Pushing on his neck. No. He shook his head but wasn't really talking to me. He seemed to be in shock. I slid my hand down his back, continuing to push. "Here?" No. "Here?" Suddenly, I became aware my hand was wet and sticky.

For years, Mrs. Amy had recited an EMS proverb I now recalled with horror, "If it's wet, sticky, and not yours, don't touch it." Uh oh. I withdrew my hand and examined it, but, in the darkness, I could see nothing. A police officer was standing over me and had taken a special interest in this kid. He directed his flashlight beam down, and I found my hand had been enveloped in an avulsed flap of skin hanging off his back. He was oblivious to the fact I was touching muscle, bone, tendon, and spine. I recoiled at the revelation and quickly shed the bloody glove, put on a new one, and applied a large trauma dressing to his back before strapping him to a long backboard. If it wasn't already, my sense of urgency had now been elevated.

The cop placed his hand on my shoulder and spoke directly into my ear, "I'm coming with you."

The ambulance doors slammed shut, and I set about the business of life saving. There were a million things to do, and for the first time, I was the one in charge when it mattered. I was being crushed beneath the weight of this monkey, and by then, I had begun to take notice of my trend of firsts. "What the hell, man?" I muttered.

Later, I realized the horrors of that scene I didn't remember. My recollections were not my own. My memory of the body in the street is from a picture we were shown in the critical incident stress debriefing that followed. This was a time to decompress and discuss our feelings on the incident. We gave our perspectives and lent support to those who needed it. We talked feelings a little to please the therapist that had been called in to lead us, and we all agreed it was messed up. However, most of us just used it as a time to talk about the grotesque details. We didn't want to be seen as weak.

The guys discussed the body in the car and how they washed a leg out of the tree with a fire hose, but they couldn't quite get all of it. There was still some up there, a grizzly reminder we would face for several days alongside the scarred tree and the roadside memorials constructed in their honor. We said we were okay, and I did feel better learning the full story I hadn't known during the fog of war. I liked knowing I wasn't the only one bothered by how horrible it all was, but I had made it through my first critical incident.

First Day at a New Job

By now you're probably thinking: "Seriously? Another one? This can't be real." Trust me, it is. I changed jobs. I couldn't take the pace of city life anymore, and I was looking for a new beginning. I was assigned to cover a small town in the middle of nowhere. The word "town" is almost laughable. There's a Dairy Queen, a Burger King, a Domino's Pizza, a gas station, a feed and seed store, a local bank that advertised easy credit for farmland, and the Town Hall—all the small-town staples that held together a place where there was nothing to do and nowhere to go.

At any given time, there were two cops on duty to cover too many miles of territory, not that they really tried. It was a speed trap town. They were usually running radar on the main drag, trying to catch the out of towners passing through from wherever they came to wherever they were going. It bolstered the town coffers, and in return they kept the cops employed.

My shift started at eight o'clock, and my new lieutenant was already waiting to give me the tour of the station. I was shown the ambulance, the station, introduced to my partner du jour, and was given a quick rundown of how the computer software worked. "You'll be fine, right?" This was a much less formal introduction than I was used to, but I thought I would be okay. It was the same as the stuff I was using back in Portsmouth, and the job couldn't have been that much different, right?

I didn't get the sense I would be doing much anyway. I was given two pieces of advice. During the tour, there was special emphasis placed on the recliners in the TV room. "Sit in them if you want. Hell, sleep in them if you want. Nobody cares." The second piece of advice I was given was to "Get used to being on your own. Help is a long way away, and there aren't many volunteers around during the day."

She left and my partner had already settled into the training room. She had brought her sewing machine and was making a quilt. She clearly didn't plan to be very busy today. I wandered around, pacing impatiently. My history of firsts nagged at me in the back of my mind. "Sit down," my partner told me. "You're making me nervous." I returned to the TV room and opened the logbook that detailed all the calls this ambulance had responded to. I reviewed the previous shift and in it, there were only two. None the day before that. This was too good to be true. It was just the sort of break I had been looking for.

I began to get comfortable with the idea this was just what happened around here. I accepted the advice of my lieutenant and determined it wasn't a trap after all. Comfortable in my new home, I plopped down in the recliner. It was well used and absorbed me. One hour into my new life as a country medic, I had fully embraced the lifestyle. This was going to be amazing. I clicked on the TV and reclined in the chair. Flipping between channels, I settled on *Modern Marvels*. It was the perfect show to lull me to sleep, and so, I closed my eyes and drifted off into dreamland.

My somnolence was short lived. I awakened to the shrill thunder of an obnoxiously loud, excessively long, rattle of an old school bell. This bell has made guest appearances in every movie about firefighting I can recall, but you don't find them in any modern station since we've long discarded them in favor of more subtle varieties that don't create as much stress on the heart. This building was anything but modern. It was 9:25. The radio crackled to life. A farm machinery accident. There it was. My streak of firsts had found me again, and this time, it could not be a more cliché initiation for a newly minted country medic.

I plugged the address into my GPS and was given a twenty-two-minute ETA. The computer said something about an amputation. These initiations were getting ridiculous. My first decision as a country medic had to be made immediately. "Do you want to launch the helicopter?" the dispatcher asked. I had an hour transport to the nearest trauma center and sixteen minutes before I even arrived on scene. I did want to launch the helicopter. This guy could have been dead before I even got there if his arm was really amputated.

I pulled up into a freshly tilled field to find a man who had fallen off the back of his planter into the turning spokes of the planter *wheel*? What was that? I didn't know. This was new to me. One of the spikes had impaled his arm and the wheel kept turning, ripping his arm off until the disembodied appendage wedged itself into the wall of the machine and brought it to a halt. The arm was still attached, but barely. He was surprisingly calm and answered all my questions as I tried to figure out how I was going to extricate him from this spikey wheel thing.

While the firefighters debated complicated extrication techniques, I could see only one solution. There was a flap of skin with a spike protruding from it. This piece of skin was the only thing preventing us from dislodging the appendage and extricating him from his predicament. I drew my shears from their holster and set about the gruesome work of cutting it away, a procedure not found in any protocol manual. What else could I do? I was on my own out there and expected to get the job done.

The arm was a lost cause, and this little strip of skin certainly wasn't going to make it any worse, so I cut it. He didn't seem to notice. In just a few moments, he was freed from the entanglement with the mangled, mostly amputated arm still attached by just a few strips of skin and some hamburgered muscle. Above me, the helicopter unceremoniously descended, bathed us in roto wash, blasted us with dirt and debris, and sank the skids into the softened earth. If you've ever wondered if paramedics have heroes, we do. Like angels, they descend from the sky and relieve us of the responsibility of care for the worst patients. My new captain arrived and slapped me on the back. "Hell of a job!" he said. I was just proud to have stood on my own and proved myself to my new peers. Then it hit me. *Did I just amputate an arm?*

First Day at a New Station

A few months into my new job, I had adapted to country medic life and the many challenges that it posed. I had made it sound so good to Captain Boz that he hung up his bugles and retired from Portsmouth to join me on the porch swing and listen to the crickets chirping at night. We used to play a game called "gunshots or fireworks?" but now the uncertainty was gone. Those distant bangs were most definitely gunshots, the chorus of good country folk dispatching a giant buck we had seen out in the cornfield earlier in the day. It suited us well.

Boz needed a day off and asked me to trade shifts with him. I had never worked at his station before, but it had a strong reputation for napping. It was the perfect place for a retired captain who had seen it all, but not so much for a younger guy. "Bring something to do, you're gonna be bored," he told me. He was right, but I hadn't listened. I expected to do what I always did, watch YouTube on my computer or phone. It was just for a day, anyway. I'd make it work.

Lesson number one of the country medic: Never assume adequate cell service. Lesson Number two: Never assume somebody will be around to tell you the Wi-Fi password. With both rules violated, I paced, and sat, and then paced some more. At last, I was overjoyed to hear the station tones. Finally, there was something to do! "Allergic reaction, Medic 20 respond," announced the dispatcher. *Great, a rash*, I thought to myself, disappointed.

On scene, I found an elderly woman lying on the floor of her living room. In broken English, her husband explained she had been swarmed by a hive of angry bees, and she was allergic. This is a classic training scenario I'd been given dozens of times throughout EMT and paramedic school but is rarely seen in the field. I had never personally encountered one, but I had rehearsed this specific call so many times that management was second nature. "Anaphylaxis, let's load and go," I recited out loud, as if I was verbalizing my way through the given scenario.

We loaded her onto the stretcher and rolled her out to the ambulance. I began thinking of all the things that needed to happen. Epinephrine to combat the effects of the vasodilation and bronchioles closing, check the body for any remaining stingers, scrape them off with a credit card if any were found, start an IV, administer Benadryl to stop the histamine reaction, albuterol to open the lung passages, solumedrol for long term inflammation, and IV fluids to maintain blood pressure. Suddenly, it occurred to me, why is she unconscious? That was never part of the scenario. I began to go through the Hs and Ts, an acronym that helps to determine the cause of unconsciousness. There are twelve of them, and they all start with H or T.

I recited them quietly to myself and began to rule them out in order of easiest to most difficult. Hypoglycemia. "Let's check her sugar," I told my partner. It came back normal. Hypoxia, Hypovolemia, and Toxins could all be covered by anaphylaxis, but her blood pressure was okay, and her oxygen levels were normal, so I wasn't convinced that was the source of her unresponsiveness. Hypo and Hyperkalemia seemed unlikely, and it was July so hypothermia wasn't a concern.

Thrombosis. Was it a blood clot in the lung, or perhaps a heart attack? Unlikely, but an EKG was easy enough to run so there was no harm in checking. We applied the EKG cables, plugged in the patient's information, and hit the print button. My partner handed it to me, and I sat it to the side without looking at it as I finished up with the IV. I taped the catheter to her arm, applied a bio-occlusive dressing, and gave the patient her arm back. I took off my gloves and picked up the printout, shocked to find the words ***MEETS STEMI CRITERIA.*** written in bold across the top.

The machine had decided she was in fact having a heart attack, but the machine can sometimes be wrong. Surely that couldn't be right. It was probably a false reading, so I took a moment and scanned the printout. It could not have been more obvious. There, in front of me, was the tell-tale "fireman's helmet," a pictorial representation of something called "ST elevation," and an indication of a patient having a massive heart attack. A bee sting heart attack, in fact.

I had never received this scenario in school, and now I had a problem. The treatment for anaphylaxis and heart attacks conflict with each other. If I gave epinephrine and albuterol as I would in anaphylaxis, I would increase the workload on the heart and could make the heart attack worse. If I applied nitroglycerine paste as I would with a heart attack, I could drop the patient's blood pressure and reduce the amount of blood coming to the heart, thereby making the heart attack and the allergic reaction worse. For the first time in my career, I had absolutely no idea what to do. I had been in situations previously where I had just needed a doctor for guidance and affirmation, but I had never had to call and say, "What should I do?" Today, I was definitely making that call.

I called the closest hospital, a "doc in a box," as we call them. They are technically a hospital but are ill equipped to handle complex, high acuity cases and hate it when you bring them one. I relayed my predicament and asked for a physician for orders. The reply came back. "Per the doctor, divert to the nearest cardiac center."

I chuckled to myself. "Negative," I replied. "Please understand that I have a patient who has been stung multiple times, is allergic to bees, is unconscious, and is having a heart attack. I am an hour from the nearest cardiac center and am six minutes from you. I am coming to you." I stood firmly.

After a pause on the frequency, the reply came. "We'll see you in a few."

I arrived and was met by a team of highly irritated nurses and an inquisitive doctor who still did not understand why I couldn't go to the cardiac center. I handed him the EKG and repeated the story. "Ohhh!" he replied, suddenly understanding my predicament. "Good call."

I watched them do their thing and hung around to ask the doctor if he had any idea as to why this cascaded in the way that it had. "No idea, man. The only thing I can think of is that the bee stings caused an increased workload on the heart and there wasn't as much blood returning to it. That coupled with airway restriction and decreased oxygen for a time period caused her to have a heart attack. Good job, though." A bee sting heart attack. Only me, and only on my first time on a new truck.

These are my firsts. They span across eighteen years, three departments, and four private ambulance services. They cross urban and rural landscapes, wealthy and desperately impoverished communities. I've worked in volunteer, career, combination volunteer/career, and private departments and services. I've served in EMS at every level, including at the First Responder, EMT-Basic, EMT-Enhanced, EMT-Intermediate, and Paramedic levels.

I met my wife on an ambulance when she was too young and dumb to know better. We started medic school together, but she quickly decided it wasn't for her, made smarter choices, and moved on to greener pastures. Her colleagues call her Dr. Davis now. As for me, I found I was pretty good at it, so I stuck around. With each new first, I again casted off the veil of uncertainty and reminded myself I was good, really good, even though some of the time I was just lucky and often more of a spectator to the show than "the man with the plan." But still, I was there, and that counts for something, I think.

How it Began

I stumbled into EMS by accident, which is not exactly the story of most of my peers. This was not a lifelong dream of mine. I wasn't hooked after watching an episode of *Emergency!* I didn't enter the profession by way of paternal lineage, and I wasn't even particularly enamored with the "hero" aesthetic. It had never even occurred to me public servants were heroes. I find the title ridiculous, and even now, when people thank me for my service, I never know what to say. "Uh, thank you," I respond awkwardly.

It has become a meme within my circles to thank each other for our service when someone comes off a little too proud of what they do. It goes a little something like this: Firefighter posts picture of himself in turnout gear on social media, standing in front of a burning house—most likely a training burn—with the caption "Just another day at the office." Other firefighter responds with "Thank you for your service." It's a riot, a real knee slapper.

To put it simply, I have always been "other firefighter." I've had pride in the job, enjoyed being seen in the uniform and telling people what I did for a living if they asked, but I've never been defined by it. It has always been "just a job." My wife jokes she married me because I didn't own a single fire department t-shirt. There is no "If you sent us to Hell, we'd put it out" sticker on the back of my truck. I don't have a Maltese Cross or Star of Life tattoo, and I can't quote a single word of the movie *Backdraft*. By almost all measures, I am a terrible firefighter.

There is a big secret in the fire and EMS job description. It comes hidden in the phrase "…and other duties as assigned." If somebody had told me the gravity of that little nugget would include duties such as laying on carpet that smells suspiciously like fourteen years of cat urine, covered in the hair of the offending animal, while roaches scurry up your sleeve as you try to intubate a heroin junkie under the judging eyes of nosey onlookers who shove iPhones in your face for internet clout, I venture to say I might have chosen a different career path. They don't tell you this stuff! I suppose it would make recruitment difficult.

Though I had come of age in the fallout of September 11th, a time where interest in becoming a firefighter was at an all-time high, even that didn't stir the desire to enter the profession. My story was much less noble. My story, like all great epochs, began with a girl. My high school girlfriend's father had a series of melted helmets hanging on his wall with a story behind each one. As he told the tales, I think he noticed I hung on every word, and he invited me to come down to his station for a recruitment open house so he could introduce me around to the guys.

In all honesty, I think he just wanted his daughter's boyfriend to have some sort of plan or demonstrated ambition before graduation, and I had none at the time. He didn't have to worry about that for long. Before I could go to the event, we broke up, and I felt it would be too awkward, so I skipped it, but the seed had been planted. I approached my high school guidance counselor, and she suggested I make contact with the local volunteer fire department and see what their recommendations were, so I did.

I showed up at the monthly business meeting and filled out an application. It was bizarre. The meeting was held in the bay between the trucks. Some folks were filthy from a hard day's work laying gas lines, and others were dressed in a suit and tie as they came from the office where they worked as an insurance agent, but they were all equal in this room and united in a common purpose—service to their community.

At my first meeting, I was startled by the bell ringing overhead, and then enamored with the paramedics who calmly stood up, pushed their chairs in, and orderly filed out with their heads down, as if they had been there, done that. There was no alarm in them, no sense of urgency. It wasn't their emergency. For them, it was business as usual and I was captivated by their demeanor.

After the meeting, the chief pulled me aside. "Come on by during the month. Let people meet you, help them out on the trucks, come have dinner. That way we'll know who we're getting when we vote to let you become a member next month," he explained. It seemed simple enough.

For the next month, when I wasn't at school, I was at the station. I was taken with the vulgarity, ribbing, and banter between the crews. It was like an entirely different language. I had never experienced people talking like that to each other, and at first, I was offended when it was directed toward me. I didn't know what to say, so I just sat there quietly and smiled awkwardly.

Later, it was explained to me that if they mess with you, it means they like you, and once I had that context, it became more comfortable. It still took me several years to develop a flair for sending it back, and only recently have I realized I initiate the new folks in the same manner, except now I recognize the smile of uncertainty. I realized I was being inducted into an elite fraternity that could only exist in circumstances where people endure hardship together. A sharp tongue and keen wit are fantastic ways to make light of an uncomfortable situation. It made sense to me.

At the next business meeting, when the time came to discuss new members, I was asked to step out of the room while they deliberated on my application. Approximately twenty minutes went by while I nervously paced the hallways before the chief broke the plane of the door. "Hey, come into my office for a second." I followed nervously.

He closed the door behind him and gave me a solemn look. "I'm sorry to inform you that the board has decided not to accept your application." I was crushed. I couldn't hide the disappointment on my face, but the chief couldn't hold the smile back on his. "I'm just kiddin.' You're in. Wipe that look off your face. You look like I killed your puppy," he said with a slap on my shoulder. "You gotta start coming to training and pullin' duty." He tossed me a shirt and just like that, I was branded with new status as a volunteer firefighter, but despite what my shirt said, I still had to earn the title. Of course, that didn't stop me from wearing the shirt.

It just so happened there was a firefighter certification class on the horizon for new members like me, and I eagerly signed up. The first classes were CPR and First Aid, the foundation for a first responder. The more I learned, the more I wanted to learn. I set up camp in one of the bunkrooms at the station and made it my semi-permanent home away from home. I estimate that fifteen to twenty nights per month were spent at the firehouse, dying for the chance to experience a house fire, which were not very abundant. What did come frequently were car accidents and EMS calls, and I never missed an opportunity to add my name to those call rosters. I was developing a passion for what I was doing, and I knew I had to make it a career.

If we're being honest, my career started much earlier than those days as a volunteer, at six years old to be precise. My mom credits me for saving my brother's life when he choked on a quarter as a baby. I "heroically" noticed he was turning an unseemly shade of blue and asked if that was normal. I found out it wasn't in the flurry of panicked activity that resulted. Did you know that turning blue could get your brother beaten? Did you know that if you hit my brother's back, he'll produce a quarter out of his mouth, like a slot machine? It seemed like a harsh punishment for a minor offense, but I guess it worked because he reverted to his normal color, and I got a quarter for my troubles.

On another occasion, mom was in the bedroom folding laundry when I vociferously attempted to inform her a pan had caught fire in the kitchen. She shrugged it off as something I had seen on the hit 90s TV show "Rescue 911." "That's nice, honey," she replied. And so I resigned to return to the couch, basking in the glow of the growing flames flickering beneath the dead kitchen smoke detector, until my dad came home from work, grabbed the pan, and ran outside with the flaming grease.

By the age of six, I had one life and one property save under my belt. On both occasions I received "attaboys," and I guess I kind of liked that feeling. However, it was not until I began legitimately serving others I was able to develop that interest and explore it further. After about six months, I completed my initial firefighter training and began applying for jobs as a firefighter. There just weren't very many to go around.

In the shadow of September 11th, firefighting was one of the most desirable careers, and as I recollect, a local department filled a coliseum three times with applicants for twelve positions. I needed a better way to achieve my goal. "Dude, get your EMT," my chief encouraged me. Depending on the department, something like 80-90 percent of calls are medical, and I realized he was right. Just about every young boy has the dream of being a firefighter at some point while growing up, but the ambulance is the oft overlooked, proverbial, redheaded stepchild. It's the necessary evil nobody really wants, but the hurdle one must over-come to be able to put the wet stuff on the red stuff. Most guys rush to fire school, and then drag their feet to EMT school like a reluctant groom to the alter. I knew if I became an EMT, I would have an advantage over the competition, so I enrolled in an EMT-Basic class.

EMS started as a hoop that I had to jump through, but there was some-thing different about it that scratched an itch I did not know I had. It was intellec-tual and mechanical, art and science, a beautiful dance between stoic professionalism and good-humored patient assurance. I recently had a patient bring a gift basket to the station to thank us for keeping them laughing even while they worried about their loved one. She said she knew her husband was in good and competent hands, and our demeanor really put her mind at ease.

I love that about this profession. Firefighting is dedicated to stopping de-struction. EMS takes that step a bit further and seeks to restore, alleviate, and heal. I was fascinated with the human body and its processes. There are so many vari-ables and inputs that work together to achieve homeostasis, the biology term for "state of normal." If even one of those variables deviates, then the mix is thrown off and, like an out of tune guitar, no matter what chord you play, none of them sound good. As an EMT, it would be my job to figure out which variable was caus-ing the problem and fix it so the body could get back to homeostasis.

As I neared completion of my training, I began an internship on the am-bulance. There was one paramedic I really looked up to named Billy. He was a white-haired man with a mustache compliment and thin rimmed glasses he wore on the tip of his nose. He wore his duty shirt neatly tucked into his tactical pants with a pair of shears tucked into his belt loop and an EMS tool kit strapped to his leather belt. Though he was nearing retirement age, he was always welcoming and didn't treat me like a nuisance, though in retrospect, I can see I probably was one. The man clearly loved this job. He never complained and treated every patient and complaint like it was the most important thing he had to do that day.

One day, as I walked out of the room after transferring a patient, he gently grabbed me by the shoulder and told me in a stern tone, "You always say goodbye to your patients. Never leave the hospital without saying goodbye." To this day, I have never left a room without wishing a patient well and telling them goodbye. Billy was a stark contrast to the majority of the paramedics I have met in my career, and I am grateful he was the first that I encountered. He gave me something to strive for. Not only was he good at what he did, but he was humble and kind.

In my experience, you can be an absolute buffoon, but if you're nice, people think that you're wonderful. As a result, I have met some fantastic paramedics, but a lot of them lack the kindness gene. I have also met some of the worst practitioners, but they are "people people" and if you asked the patients to rank them, the dumb ones would score higher. I doubt this is unique to medicine. My guess is that it probably translates across professions. Kindness does a much better job at covering ineptness than does the inverse. The combination of kindness and exceptional ability is a rare combination, and therefore, when you encounter these folks, they are considered elite. Billy was elite, and it has been my career long pursuit to be just like him.

Having said that, I look back at Billy now in wonder. How did that man maintain his "eliteness" while I sometimes struggle to even get out of bed on the mornings I have to go to work? How did he keep his positive attitude over thirty plus years? I asked Billy when he was going to retire once. "I don't know. I haven't really thought about it. I guess when I don't love it anymore." After all those years, Billy still loved it and couldn't imagine stopping.

Today, *I* wonder if I have the wherewithal to keep going. I look in the mirror and, at thirty-six years old, I feel and look old. My once thick and dark hair has thinned and fallen away from my forehead. What's left is salt and pepper, with more salt than pepper these days. My eyes are sunken and bloodshot with dark circles framing them. I look tired. I *am* tired and burnt out, and I know that I am not alone.

The Journal for Emergency Medical Services (JEMS) reports a study on EMS burnout found 60 percent of providers "strongly agree" with the statement "I feel burned out in my EMS work," while 28 percent somewhat agree. That is 88 percent of EMS providers who feel burned out, at least to some degree. Thirty-six percent report wanting to leave the field entirely while still more somewhat agree they want to change careers. The caveat is that all of those statistics were taken in a pre-COVID world. I bet it would be even worse if they sent the survey out now.

In a recent article in *EMS World Magazine*, it was revealed that 15.5 percent of firefighters have attempted to take their own life at least once in their careers, and 27.2% of EMS providers have contemplated suicide in the last year—a rate seven times higher than the national average. In a study of 903 EMS providers taking the Suicidal Behaviors Questionnaire-Revised (SBQ-R), it was found that 31.3 percent of EMS providers scored a seven or higher, reflecting increased risk for future suicide. I took it and scored a nine at the time of this writing.

Statistics provide the scientific backing, but sometimes we need a picture painted beyond the numbers. These are some comments from medics and health-care providers I have read on various social media pages in the last year. Beware, some of them are a bit raw and names or screennames have been withheld for privacy reasons. In response to a question on Reddit from a prospective EMT about how EMS has affected your homelife, the following answer was given:

[I've] been a 911 big city third-service street medic for 6 years. The sheer amount of untethered stupidity has made me hate everyone, despise working and want to suck off a shotgun, but at least I've tried some really sweet new types of whiskey and I know where all the homeless shelters are for when my poverty level income inevitably stops being enough to support the ever-increasing cost of rent. Too bad going back to school to do anything else is a pipe dream. Speaking of which, PLEASE choose LITERALLY any other career. Go be a McDonalds manager for all I care. Don't go to EMT school or you'll be stuck here wasting your mind and body away like the rest of us salty assholes.

I am tired. I sit in my car before every shift and cry at the thought of walking into the ER for 12 hours.

A patient told me that I have no idea what it's like to be suicidal. I'm sorry, buddy, but you have no idea how wrong you are.

Wake up and realize your thin white line has cracked. Most of us are drowning. Healthcare is in trouble people.

If I asked for a quote from every provider I know, I could probably write a separate book for just these quotes. These are a pretty good summary of the col-lective feeling these days, but it goes even deeper.

We have given title to the phenomenon of divorce that occurs within our field, Ambulance Induced Divorce Syndrome (AIDS). Look it up—it's a real thing.

At one point in my career, I was in a station with ten guys who had all been divorced. That small sampling was 100 percent, but at least within that department, we weren't unique. When I came into the fire service, I remember a veteran firefighter named Frank asking me if I was married. When I said yes, he told me, "That'll change." He was right. In fact, he was almost right twice.

The fact of the matter is that this job can suck a whole bunch. The rewards are few and far between, and I'm not just talking about the money and thank yous. I'm talking about the satisfaction of being able to do what you know you have the ability to do, saving lives. The calls where you can actually make a difference are rare. I can probably count on two hands the number of people who are still alive today directly as a result of something that I have done. The rest of my time is spent taxiing people to the hospital for complaints that are often trumped in severity by whatever ache or ailment that *I* am feeling. These are complaints that should have been managed at home with Tylenol or just toughing it out, which is a skill that seems to be lost. We've become a society of lazy, entitled children with expectations of an instant remedy for whatever ails us. It doesn't work like that, and three hours of vomiting doesn't warrant an ambulance ride or taking up a hospital bed. I would love to see a societal reckoning on this.

In addition to the lack of reward in job satisfaction, there is serious depravity in financial reward as well. I have never complained about the pay as I have always felt I was compensated well in my organizations, but there are jurisdictions out there still paying paramedics at a rate beneath the poverty line for their respective areas. The hours are long, the vacation days few, and the opportunities limited. Long nights of broken sleep completely destroy our circadian rhythms, and consequently, our bodies. We live on coffee, fast food, and Motrin. There is no work life balance because most of us work multiple jobs to make ends meet on top of the fifty-three-hour minimums we're working at our full-time jobs.

Even if we did work only one job, we couldn't go anywhere to refresh because, in much of the country, the vacation days aren't enough to actually take a real vacation. It takes at least two days of travel to get anywhere. This is my soap box. When I bring it up, I am told, "Well you can trade shifts." My partner today has traded shifts, which means she is working a forty-eight-hour shift on an ambulance where she has the very real possibility of being awake for forty-eight straight hours and is still expected to be able to function and make life and death decisions. This is not safe.

Studies have shown that twenty-four hours awake is equivalent to having a blood alcohol content of 0.8. Most administrations have no qualms with allowing us to double that. We are frustrated by what the population thinks our job is and what it actually is and how nonchalantly they shrug it off when we educate them. We are disgusted with the way people live, how they treat each other, and the horrible things they are capable of doing to others, but nothing surprises us anymore. Most of us entered this field because we wanted to make a difference, but lately it just doesn't feel like we're doing that. Most of us have ideas to move the profession forward to fill an obvious gaping hole, but we are often stymied by stagnant minded leadership who struggle to move past "the way we've always done it" and antiquated medical billing practices. We are serving the need that *was*, and not the need that *is*. We know that change is needed, but when we voice that, it nearly always falls on deaf ears.

In the last five years, I have noticed a new phenomenon. People aren't actually becoming paramedics to be paramedics. It's a stepping-stone to get somewhere else. Most of them want to be doctors, physician's assistants, or nurses and view it as a way to gain experience before they apply to their respective programs. I used to ask, "What made you want to get into EMS?," but after a few awkward, silent moments, I learned to ask, "Is this your end goal or are you planning to move on to something else?" I haven't been told that this is the end goal in several years.

Nobody is sticking around, and there are a lot of good reasons not to. According to the National Registry of Emergency Medical Technicians (NREMT), half of all EMTs are volunteer. Can you think of another job in medicine in which the expectation is free labor with the promise of *maybe* being paid later? Can you think of another job, period, with an educational requirement that has a prerequisite of volunteer service? Paramedics are more frequently employed, but there is still a segment of the country that asks for free work from paramedics as well.

Virginia Beach comes to mind. They are the largest "all volunteer" rescue squad in the nation, serving a population of 450,000 people. While in recent years they have employed paramedics to supplement the holes left by volunteers who have to work real jobs to support themselves, the bulk of the labor force remains volunteer. This is a source of frustration for me. How can you demand fair pay when you're competing against free? Why do we do this to ourselves? I would ask why this is expected of us, but we can't really complain when we do it willingly, right? Whether out of sense of duty, service to community, hope of gaining experience, expectation of getting a job, excitement, exploration of new career, or whatever the case may be, we are not doing ourselves any favors. I'm just as guilty as everyone else. Volunteering is where I got my feet wet as well, but if we are ever to be taken seriously as a profession, then we must demand better for ourselves.

Chapter 4

HEART

I have been underestimated my entire life. At an adult height of 5'6", I have always been at least a full head shorter than most of my peers, so when I showed up to the fire department physical agility test, a scrawny, 110 pound, eighteen-year-old kid, I was not shocked by the looks exchanged between the instructors that said, "this should be quick." I don't mind those looks. In fact, I have grown to love them because it means the bar is set at the floor, and whatever I do from this moment is more than was expected. I thrive in these moments, because as a kid, I was let in on a little secret.

My first love was baseball. I played it, I watched it, ate, slept, and breathed it. The problem was that for all my passion, it meant absolutely nothing at the beginning of every season. I was the kid that garnered shouts of, "Move in, guys!" as I stepped up to the plate and was always sent to right field where the worst players in little league are hidden. I had to work twice as hard to prove I could cut it. One afternoon, frustrated by my relegation to obscurity in little league Hell, I vented my frustrations to my dad.

"Why won't they just give me a chance? I can't help that I'm short," I asked.

"You just have to prove yourself, kiddo. Use your height to your advantage."

I thought about that for a moment. How was I supposed to do that?

At my next game, batting toward the bottom of the order, I thought back to my dad's words as I stepped up to the plate. Surveying the field, I watched the infielders moving into position at the edge of the infield grass and the outfielders filling in the gaps around them. The pitcher stepped onto the mound with a smirk of certainty on his face. I could read his mind—"Easy out, guys." I dug my back foot into the box and settled in as he came set on the mound. As the wind up began, I sank into an exaggerated squat. My twenty-four-inch strike zone shrank to about sixteen inches. The pitcher released the ball, and it sailed high, a foot over my head. Ball one. "What is he doing?" my coach asked my dad. Dad laughed.

"Just watch," he said.

As the pitcher toed the rubber once more, I settled into my squat and waited. Trying to compensate for the height of the last pitch, he released late, and the ball skipped off the dirt four feet in front of the plate. Ball two. The arrogant smirk had departed from his stupid face and found its way to mine. The catcher tossed the ball back, and he caught it, swinging his glove hand wildly, visibly frustrated. He circled the mound to collect himself, and after a moment, mounted the rubber once more.

Baseball is a mental game, and I was in his head. I wasn't about to let up now. It was the time to increase the pressure. I had already taken away the top and bottom of the zone, now it was time to take the inside. I slid closer to the plate so that my oversized jersey hung over the edge. If he was going to throw an inside strike, it was going to hit me. We repeated the song and dance, and as the next pitch came in, it barreled toward my head. I fell out of the box and the ball sailed past a diving catcher to the backstop. Ball three. He looked to the dugout and shrugged his shoulders. With an ingenious piece of advice, his coach chimed in. "Don't worry about it! Just throw strikes."

"He has no strike zone!" the kid yelled back.

I dusted myself off and retook my place at the edge of the plate, this time not waiting to sink into my squat. There was nothing to hide anymore. I could hear my coach laughing behind me. With the next pitch, it sailed wildly three feet outside. The catcher didn't even try to catch it and took his time standing up to retrieve the ball. I sprinted toward first base and rounded it. Suddenly realizing that the play was live, the catcher kicked it into gear and grabbed the ball, flinging it in the direction he thought was second base. It wasn't.

The ball sailed wildly into left field, and I rounded second toward third. The left fielder collected the ball and fired toward the hot corner. It skipped in just as I slid into the bag in a cloud of dust. Popping up, I dusted myself off, but I suddenly realized the entire crowd was screaming at me. "GO! GO! GO!" shouted my third base coach, jumping around wildly and swinging his arm in circles, willing me toward home plate. I looked around and realized I was standing alone on third base. The third baseman was running toward the fence where the ball had skipped away.

I took off running again and crossed the plate just ahead of the throw. I had turned a walk into a little league homerun thanks to a little squat, some gamesmanship, and heads up baserunning. But more importantly, I had deflated the opposing team. From that day on, my coach realized I could get on base almost every time, and I started batting lead-off. I also got a few more opportunities to swing the bat since the pitchers just focused on throwing it right down the middle, and in the field, I eventually settled in behind the plate as a catcher, where my short stature was an asset. I found my place.

Fast forward to the fire academy. I did myself no favors on that first day. It was cold outside, and I had one jacket—my bright yellow work jacket with silver reflective lettering on it that said "Medical Transport"—so I wore it. If the goal was to keep my head down and remain inconspicuous, I should have gone sleeveless. The instructor clearly took it as a sign of arrogance, as if I was saying, "I don't need this job. I already have a job."

As we huddled in the waiting room of fire headquarters awaiting instructions, he walked in at a brisk pace and stopped dead in his tracks. The neon glow of my jacket had made the hairs on his drill instructor neck stand erect. He turned and his gaze fixated on me, remaining silent for a moment as I smiled awkwardly back at him, uncertain what to do or say. "What the fuck is your name?" he demanded.

"Um, Chad," I responded timidly.

"Is 'um' your first name?" he asked.

"No," I replied.

"No, what?"

"It's not my first name," I said uncomfortably.

"Then why the fuck did you say it was?"

"Chad is my first name," I replied.

"I don't give a fuck about your first name! What is your last name?" he shouted.

"Davis, sir."

He thought for a moment. "No, your name is Tiny. Now take that shit off. This isn't medical transport!" he said, turning and disappearing through the doorway of the office, leaving me sitting once again in silence. I could feel every eye in the room on me as I obeyed the order to remove my jacket.

Later, we lined up on the PT ground and were taught the basic commands of the fire academy, such as "Attention on Deck" and "At Ease." We then got our first taste of PT. Did I mention I had the flu? I should *not* have been at work, but I had been told I could not miss even one day of the fire academy or they would fire me. So I showed up, febrile, coughing, and miserable.

"Push-ups!" shouted the instructor. I fell to my face and got to three before I felt the contents of my stomach begin to churn. Shaking, I completed the exercise and remained in the plank position until the order to "Recover" came. I struggled to my feet and fought the urge to vomit. "Mountain climbers!" I could feel myself turning green as I fell to my face once again and raised up on my hands and toes, butt in the air, and began to repeatedly knee myself in the stomach. The queasiness became overwhelming, and I had to stop. The instructor, unaware of my illness, ran over and got into my face. "What is your problem, Tiny? We're not taking breaks! We're going to do this until one of you throws up!"

Right on cue, the churn within erupted, and for the moment, I felt better and resumed my mountain climbers. The instructor backed away and laughed. "Never mind! We're going to do this until all of you throw up!" he shouted, clearly annoyed at my stomach's challenge to his authority. Within that first day, I had established myself as weak, rebellious, and arrogant, and all I had done was show up in a yellow jacket with the flu.

On day two, they sorted us into squads, which for me was a lot like being picked last in dodgeball. The first two squads consisted of the ripped dudes with the chiseled jaws and 2 percent body fat. I didn't make it into that squad. Squads three and four consisted of the middle of the pack folks. Their jaws weren't quite as chiseled, and their mile was probably a minute or two longer, but those guys weren't getting picked last.

When squad five was assembled, I looked to my left and then to my right. Standing next to me were a forty-two-year-old man with knee braces, a nerdy looking dude with a little extra pudge, and, as I would soon find out, an excuse for every failure, and another guy who looked pretty normal. I am not sure why they put him in this squad, but if I had to guess, it was his known association with the volunteer rescue squads in Virginia Beach, who had a local reputation for being "para-gods." I'm assuming they felt they would need to bust him down a notch, so here he stood with the rest of us rejects. We were very clearly ranked based on first impressions, and so formed squad five.

Once formed, we were introduced to the twenty-first recruit of Class Thirty-Nine, Recruit Dong. Yes that really was his name but let me explain. Recruit Dong was not a person but a bell nailed to piece of wood. He served three purposes. The first was taken from Navy SEAL BUDS training. If ever we wanted to stop doing whatever uncomfortable thing we were doing at the time, all we had to do was stand up, walk up to Dong, ring him, and we could stop. We also got to stop all other activities in the fire academy because to ring Dong meant you were quitting.

The second purpose that Recruit Dong served was in remembrance of the firefighters who had fallen in the line of duty during the week. Each Monday we would read off their names one by one and ring Dong once in their honor. This tradition signifies their last call and would be followed by a moment of silence in their memory. This was to serve as a stoic reminder of the dangers of the career we had chosen and was intended to keep our minds focused on the task at hand. Train like your life depends on it, because in this career, it does.

Finally, the third purpose of Recruit Dong was much less noble. It probably seems strange I have humanized a bell at this point, but that was the way we were taught to think of him. Each morning, at role call, we were to include him in our par count. We were accountable for him, as we were for each other, at every moment of every day. He was to remain with us always, and the responsibility for carrying him fell to the worst squad of the week.

The caveat was Dong had to remain silent at all times because to hear his ring meant someone's career had ended, either tragically, or because they had simply given up. The instructors intended to keep the metaphor sacred, so we guarded the bell and walked with his clapper muffled in the palm of our hands. The instructors enjoyed making a game of this and would try to catch us napping, running up and ringing the bell when nobody was holding it. If the bell sounded, punishment ensued. This usually took the form of pushups or the "magic chair."

This form of torture should be banned by the Geneva Convention but is good enough for fire recruits. It required us to place our backs against the wall and drop our legs to a ninety-degree angle, like we were sitting in an invisible chair, and extend our arms straight out in front of us. The pain this caused in the quadriceps and shoulders was intense and was an exercise of extreme endurance. They would leave us in this position for ten to fifteen minutes, sometimes leaving to do other things while our bodies shook in agony, only to come back and say, "Oh, you guys can recover." Recovery was usually impossible as my legs had changed their state of matter and now had more in common with Jell-O than human propulsion devices. Oh, how I *disdained* the magic chair.

I mentioned Dong was given to the worst squad of the week. The eye test used to rank us on that first day was affirmed by the physical challenges used to rank us through the rest of the academy. Each week we would work through a PT exam or skill test and would be timed. The first day eye test proved to be pretty accurate as Squad Five was last almost every week.

At the beginning of the academy, each squad was given an axe and a Halligan bar, called a set of "Irons," when paired together. A Halligan bar is a rod with a two-pronged fork on one end and an L-shaped spike and flat bar on the other. In skilled hands, this set of tools can get through nearly any locked door. There were four sets of irons, but five squads. The fifth set of irons consisted of an axe and a goofy tool named the hooligan bar, which was a fitting name for a tool that doesn't serve a purpose. It can't do anything that a Halligan can't do. It is essentially just a Halligan bar but about a foot longer, which makes pairing it with the axe impossible since the handle of the axe wasn't long enough to fit neatly into the angle of the L-shaped end, called the "adze." To carry them together, they had to be tied, and they frequently fell apart as we tried to move quickly, putting us further behind the rest of our group as we tried to piece the puzzle back together.

This set was painted pink and was given to the worst squad of the week along with Recruit Dong. Squad Five became known as the "Pink Iron Squad" as they remained in our possession for all but confined space week, which I am proud to say was because I excelled at fitting in tight spaces. Remember my baseball story? I found my niche and my size became an advantage. Everything on the fireground is heavy, and I had to work twice as hard to do the same job as the others, but if there was someone that needed to go through a tiny hole, Recruit Tiny was the guy for the job.

As it turned out, in the structure of the academy, I was in my element. It is designed to test your preconceived notions about your abilities. When it got hard, that's when they were watching. Everything was measured. Everything was timed. Everything was competitive. If you weren't competing against others, you were competing against yourself. If you met the goal, you pushed others. If you weren't meeting the goal, others were pushing you, because nobody wanted to carry those pink irons.

I found myself pushing more than needing to be pushed, particularly within my squad. I decided I could do one more of anything or do anything for just one more minute. When the pain of the magic chair was too much to bear, I would tell myself, "Just one more minute." When that minute passed, I again told myself I just had to do one more minute. Pretty soon, I was five minutes beyond when my legs told me it was time to quit.

Every Thursday we completed a six-mile run. While most things in the academy were a team event that required a partner, the run was an individual event. I loved Thursdays. I set my pace and, each week, strove to push myself beyond it. Pretty soon I was running eight and a half-minute miles and finishing at the front of my class. When I finished, I turned and ran the two miles back to pick up the stragglers in my squad and "motivated" them toward the finish line. This meant while I was required to run six miles, I was running ten and dragging my team along with me. The instructors had begun to take notice.

This carried over into live fire training. The drill was to go into the building and seek out the fire. We would split into teams of two, and one would extinguish the fire while the other team was assigned to search out and rescue the victim from the building. I was assigned to the latter.

Under the guise of "testing" us, some overzealous younger instructors heated the building well past the design limitations. At 1,400 degrees at the ceiling level, the heat was so intense it cracked the heat resistant tiles. I made the mistake of grabbing the metal stair railing, which instantly seared my hand through the protective fire glove. Ignoring the urge to panic, I continued up the stairs, careful not to grab onto the rail again, but in the darkness and smoke, my shoulder brushed against it, and again I felt the sting of the red-hot steel penetrating my gear.

By now, the extinguishment team had located the fire, and there was some alarm from the lead instructors at the rising level of heat, so the extinguishment team was directed to put the fire out immediately and cool the building. The smoke and steam darkened the limited visibility we had left. We continued up the stairs and located the victim, beginning the arduous task of moving the rigid 150-pound mannequin toward the exit.

As I fumbled in the dark to grab hold of his rigid plastic body, the pressurized air hose attached to my air regulator became tangled around the dummy's arm, and as my partner moved forward, he gave a hard yank, and I lost control of the torso. Suddenly, the seal on my mask broke away from my face, and the air began free flowing around the edges. Realizing I was in trouble, the interior instructor tapped me on the shoulder and told me to leave the structure. I scurried down the stairs to be met by the lieutenant outside. "What are you doing, Davis? Where is your partner?" he screamed at me.

"They sent me down, sir. My mask broke."

Realizing the problem, he guided me through the remedy and told me to, "Get your ass back in there, and help your partner!"

"Yes, sir!" I screamed and scurried back up the stairs.

Once safely back in the classroom, we held a PIA, or post incident analysis. The lieutenant recapped my scenario and explained it would have been easy to panic, but I had kept a level head and ran right back in once I had solved the problem. "You've got a lot of heart, Davis! A lot of heart!" he declared, seeming to realize at last they had mischaracterized me in the beginning.

In the moment, it was a source of pride for me, but now, all these years later, I realize it was one of the best compliments I could have been paid. I'm sure you have at least a rudimentary understanding of the phrase, but for context, I will explain it. The common understanding of the idiom is to say that someone has courage, determination, or fortitude. Can you imagine a firefighter or paramedic who is not defined by these characteristics? For being one who was relegated to the castaway squad, declared unfit, and set aside for discharge until such time as I proved their characterization incorrect, this phrase was a declaration that I had earned my place amongst their ranks. I was a firefighter.

Chapter 5

A Pain Like No Other

The mind is a puzzling thing. It is simultaneously fragile and durable. For some, it perseveres for a lifetime without ever taking a detour off the rails, while for others, it slams into a wall overnight, often without explanation. Still others straddle the fence perpetually, doing the delicate dance between completely sane and off their rocker. And some…some just get tired.

This is the category that I fell into. I have lain awake at night wondering how I went from zealous, young EMT who couldn't wait to hear the bell, to disgruntled Paramedic who curses the tones and throws my pillow at the wall when they sound. I can't identify a call or single event that stole my joy, but I can identify a turning point.

It's been a tough career, but until recently, I couldn't point to an incident and say, "That haunts me." Most of the time, I don't even know I was bothered until it makes itself known to me. It shows up as I tell the story, often for the hundredth time, but this time, something is different. When I get to the good part, the blood and gore everyone wants to hear about, I suddenly can't talk about it. I choke back the tears, unaware of where they came from. This memory has never bothered me before, but today, I guess it does. I end the story with, "Well you get the picture," and my audience is disappointed. I wonder what happened, and I file it in the "do not talk about anymore" file.

There's something about aging that changes the way you reflect on things. There's something about life that gives you a new perspective to reflect upon and a new frame of reference for those experiences. The truth is that I have Post Traumatic Stress Disorder (PTSD), but I don't wake up in a cold sweat, punching my wife, and screaming like the characters of those comically bad TV shows and movies. My kind of PTSD manifests in a short temper, quiet reflection, fleeting memories, and random triggers that transport me back to some call I've been on or tragic experience I've endured.

The calls one would think would bother me often don't, while more benign encounters cross my mind often. I believe I am adjusted to dealing with it, and I feel individual mental traumas contribute very little to the moral injury, but the collective experience of it all is one big mountain I have to scale every single day I wake up. To better explain what I mean, I want to use this chapter to talk about the intersection of my life and career and attempt to demonstrate how these events can wear on a person over time. My experiences are obviously my own, but they should paint a clear picture of the problems and frustrations I have encountered and why I have arrived at the conclusions I have. I should also note that life and career are not linear. They run parallel, sometimes overlap, and intermingle, particularly in public safety where coworkers are almost indistinguishable from family. This is a point administrators would do well to remember.

This story starts in the middle because it is the lens I view my early career through and the foundation for everything else that came after. On May 5, 2014, I was ten years into my career, married for the second time, with two children and one on the way. I will let my words from that evening introduce you this part.

> *Today was supposed to be a good day. Today we were going to announce to the world that we were expecting our third child, and as we witnessed the blip of the heartbeat on the ultrasound for the first time, my precious son, Brayden's heart stopped beating. Many of you are already aware and have absolutely gone above and beyond to dump your support on us and we want you to know that it means the world to us. There are no words you can say or things you can do to heal this pain, but we certainly appreciate your sympathy. Thank you to the Suffolk Fire Department for your efforts. I know it's hard when it's a child and even harder when it's one of your own. We don't know what to do, how to act, where to go and right now, we are leaning on each other. I know the instinct is to try to ease the burden when tragedy happens, but we would really appreciate our space for the evening and tomorrow. Thank you.*
> *-Chad Davis, Facebook, May 5, 2014*

"I can't imagine." I had uttered those words at least a dozen times after a difficult call in which a child had died. We would discuss it for a few minutes between ourselves and then tuck it away and play video games or watch a movie to bury the memory. Compartmentalization is a skill that is essential for someone who does this job because if you can't shed the memories, the faces, or the sights, sounds, or smells, you can't continue to do what we do. When I was young, I didn't find it that difficult, particularly prior to having kids. After having kids, it was a little harder, and I would say things like, "It just makes you want to go home and hug your kids a little tighter." After you lose a child, compartmentalization of that event becomes impossible.

Now, eight years later, I can remember the words I wrote as vividly as I feverishly typed them, tears streaming down my face, sitting on the couch of a cold hotel room with my grieving wife sleeping restlessly next to me. We couldn't bear to return home and see the reminders of what was now gone, and so Captain Boz had graciously rented us a room to spare us the heartache. I was exhausted, but this was the first moment I had had all day to reflect and grieve for myself and not simply be there to hold my wife while she cried. I was grateful for the reprieve and thankful she was now escaping our new reality, if even for a moment. I hoped that my chance would come to do the same, but over the next few hours, I would wrestle with a time sensitive decision that would put us at odds.

Lifenet, the organ donation network, had called and asked us to donate our precious son's organs. I do not envy that job. I stepped out of the room so she would not hear me. "Can I just do so without her consent? I can't ask that of his mother right now," I asked.

"No, unfortunately not. We have to have the consent of both parents," she replied.

I did not want to wake her, and I did not want to have this conversation at that moment, but nonetheless, the Lifenet representative explained the matter was time sensitive and gave me a twenty-four-hour deadline to make the decision. I agreed, and we ended the call. I paced the halls and weighed the decision to ask her for about an hour before I decided I needed this. I needed his life to matter for something, but when I approached Emily, the response was as expected. "No! He was my son! Those are his organs, and I don't want them cutting him up!" she angrily responded.

My response was less than graceful and nothing that a grieving mother should ever have to hear. "They're going to cut him up anyway. They have to do an autopsy!"

Fortunately for me, her best friend, Britney, had arrived and shooed me away, taking over the consolation effort. I returned to the hallway and looked out the window at the world below. I could see the highway from my vantage point and something horribly painful struck me. Traffic kept moving, restaurant employees busied themselves taking out the trash and sweeping the parking lot in preparation for closing. They just kept going with the mundane tasks of their lives. It was odd to me that none of these people had any knowledge of my son's death. It did not affect their lives in any way while my entire world had come crashing down. I couldn't blame them. How many times had I done exactly that, even knowing a mother was at home grieving the loss of her child, a child *I* had pronounced dead? How many times had I gone back to the station to finish a cold lunch after just such a moment, without ever giving it another thought?

"Chad needs this. He needs to know that Brayden's death will count for something, and if you give permission, Brayden could save other babies' lives just like you and Chad do every day. Other parents will never have to feel like you do right now. He will be a little hero."

In retrospect, that was better than my response, and Emily agreed. Thank God for Britney. With that burden off my mind, I was finally able to escape reality with Emily, but throughout the night, we awoke several times to the realization our baby had not cried for his feedings or diaper changes, only to realize this terrible dream was not a dream at all. There was no baby to cry anymore. Our child was dead. With a baby in the home, the nights are long, but when the baby suddenly isn't there anymore, they get so much longer.

The details of the morning, I don't recollect. It was just like any other day, and generally not the kind of day that ends up in a book, but I relive this day through the lens of history just as people do September 11th or the Kennedy Assassination. I think about the moments leading up to the call, when I was totally unaware of the tragedy lurking just around the corner. This is something I have thought about often. You wake up with no idea your life is about to change, or in some cases, end. I have often wondered what goes through a person's mind in the final hours, minutes, or seconds before tragedy happens. What were they thinking or worried about? What plans were they making? Who were they angry with or what menial day-to-day task was occupying their minds? What was stressing them that would no longer be a concern in just a few moments? It is something that the era of social media has allowed me to investigate more freely.

Over the years I have searched countless victims of these tragedies on social media to learn more about who they were. Perhaps it is unprofessional, unethical, or even counterproductive. I don't know if anyone else does this, but the evidence suggests they do based on the number of friend requests I received from people I didn't know after Brayden's death. To be clear, I have never inserted myself into the family's lives in that way, but I do feel my obsessive investigations allow me to keep the humanity of the people I serve in perspective and not just see the damage to their broken bodies.

Each of them had dreams, ambitions, friends, mothers, children, jobs, and ultimately just wanted good things to happen to them, until something bad happened that ended it all. I search for clues sometimes. Did a cryptic Facebook post allude to their impending suicide? Did they just post a photo on Instagram a few moments before they collided with the back of a semi-truck? Was this duck-faced, peace sign selfie responsible for their death? Were they happy in that photo? I hope their final moments were happy.

The search for reason in the death of my son was no different, although perhaps not as freely accessible since babies don't tend to tell you much or leave an online footprint. What did I miss? What did the doctors miss? It was only a week prior he had seen his pediatrician. Were the warning signs present then? There had to be something. The morning of his passing, I was the last one to wake up. Caia, my daughter from a previous marriage, was getting ready for school and Emily was getting Brayden ready to go to the babysitter. We had just learned we were pregnant again with our third child and had an appointment that morning with her obstetrician for an ultrasound.

She laid Brayden next to me, and I threw my arm over him. She snapped a picture of that moment. It was three hours before our lives would change. He was smiling and kicking his legs, and I pretended to be asleep but couldn't completely hide the smile on my face. I have studied that photo endlessly looking for any sign something was amiss, but for all my examination, I have found nothing.

There are other photos from a few weeks prior, some at Britney's wedding. He had his little suit on, was crying inconsolably, and we realized we had forgotten his formula at home. There was no grocery store for more than an hour, so we stopped at a gas station and bought some milk to fill his stomach until we could get back to civilization and buy some formula. He later spit it up on his suit and had to be changed at the reception. Was this a red flag? Should we have taken him to the doctor? No. Babies spit up. There was nothing, no warning.

I had been assigned jury duty for the month of April into May and had settled into my routine of calling to make sure I was not supposed to appear for the day. I had been fortunate to not be selected, but when I received a call from the fire station asking if I was in trouble, I realized I had forgotten to check in with the court that morning. "A police officer called here looking for you. She wants you to call her," he said, relaying the number she had left.

"Oh, no," I told Emily. "I think I missed jury duty." I wish that it had only been that.

I called, and the voice on the other end said, "Are you the father of Brayden Davis?"

My initial reaction was relief that I had not missed jury duty, but then my heart sank immediately. "Yes," I replied shakily.

The voice on the other end was somber. "You need to go to the hospital."

"Is everything okay?" I asked.

"I can't say. You just need to go to the hospital, okay?"

I ended the call and told Emily the officer's directions, and she immediately panicked. The drive to the hospital was only about seven minutes, but I probably made it in three. I can only imagine what other drivers were thinking as I passed on the shoulders, tailgated bumpers, blew through red lights without looking, and accelerated and braked without regard. I tried keeping her calm by telling her it was probably just a broken arm or something, not believing it myself.

Emily franticly attempted to contact nurses she knew at the hospital, and when she finally made contact with the nurse manager, she begged for information but was simply told, "Emily, you know that I can't give you that information. We'll talk when you get here." We knew from experience that answer meant our hope for a minor injury was fading, but I began praying for a simple coma he would be able to recover from.

We've got hard choices to make and a long road ahead of us, but he will survive whatever this is, I told myself.

The doors of the ER flew open. We didn't have to explain ourselves. They knew who we were and why we were there. We were met at the entrance by a team of nurses who said nothing. They simply held their hands over their mouths, holding back tears. The nurse manager stepped forward and directed us to his room. Nothing could have prepared me for the sight of my son lying there lifeless, endotracheal tube still protruding from his mouth, but everything was already disconnected. I remember thinking, *Why aren't you doing something? Do something!*

I looked back at the nurse manager as I fell to my knees. "He's gone," she said.

Gone? What do you mean gone? He's right here! I thought, looking back to him. I fell over the end of the bed as an uncontrollable wail left my throat. We call it the death wail and generally only hear it when a parent learns of their child's death. It's distinct. *Dead, you're supposed to say dead,* I whispered. We learn and even practice informing the family of the death of a loved one in paramedic school. They had drilled it into me so many times. You're supposed to say dead or died—a word of finality that lets the family know that there are no further options. It is such an uncomfortable word to say, and I have used dozens of euphemisms over the years to avoid the task. He's passed. He's gone. There is nothing more we can do. She is no longer with us. Anything to make it easier on myself, but I never understood these euphemisms actually do more damage than using the dreaded "D" word. I understand now.

I looked up to see my sobbing wife rocking our lifeless baby, burying her face into his. "He's my baby boy. My precious baby boy," she repeated over and over again. I do not know how long that continued, but it was more than I could bear. I wanted to vomit. I asked her if I could hold him, and she stood to give him to me, but I had become so used to him being able to hold his own head up that when she handed him to me, I failed to support it, and it flopped backwards. It was the final confirmation for me and sealed my understanding that my child was dead. It was such a terrible, sickening, and embarrassing moment that I could not stomach it. I wanted to be anywhere but in that room.

I placed him back on the bed, turned the tears off, and escorted Emily out, where we were led to the quiet room. In fifteen minutes, I had gone through several stages of grief. From denial to bargaining to anger, then back to denial, to sadness and finally to acceptance. I inherently understood my role was in support of my wife and had several men reiterate that to me over the next few days. "You are hurting, but she's that child's mother. You need to be there for her to lean on."

In retrospect, that was damaging advice and a thought process that probably led to some negative things I will discuss later.

We sat there in silence, not knowing what to do, before I finally spoke. "No matter what, we will get through this together." She did not say anything, but her silence was as good as a blood signature on that pact. We have since credited this simple pledge with the preservation of our marriage because the coming months and years were *hard,* and we drew on this promise often. We knew the statistics on marriage after the loss of a child were not in our favor. There was one study that indicated bereaved parents were up to eight times more likely to divorce than parents who have not undergone such tragedy. Other studies have challenged this assertion, citing the difficulties with tracking divorce rates over time and the limited sample size. In reality, little is known about the mental health and relationships of the bereaved after they leave the hospital. In our case, I am not sure either of us would have even survived without the other as nobody else could have understood what we were going through.

I realized I needed to start making notifications and returned to the car to retrieve my phone, which I had left in my haste to get into the building. One of the ER techs escorted me, and I heard footsteps approaching from behind me. "Do you want to talk to the medic that took care of Brayden?" he asked.

"No," I replied, but I turned anyway.

I knew most of the local firefighters and medics and was fearful it would be someone I would not have wanted working on my family. We all have colleagues we trust more than others. I was relieved when I realized it was a medic I highly respected. Hearing my answer, he had already turned to leave, but when he saw me turn, he stopped in his tracks. I walked back and embraced him and thanked him as he broke down. "I'm sorry. I'm so sorry," he said.

Over the next several months, I learned Brayden was one of several babies that had passed under his care, and it was evident it was taking a toll on him. Soon after, he took an extended vacation to clear his mind after dealing with this string of terrible calls. Unfortunately, most of our outcomes are poor when it comes to cardiac arrest. We are fighting to preserve an exceedingly miniscule chance at survival with a generally best-case scenario being an anoxic brain injury. With all of these child fatalities, I always felt guilty that Brayden's death might have tipped the scale just a bit more. I don't know this to be true, but I am positive it would have if it were me.

The hospital chaplain approached me before I made it back to the quiet room. "Excuse me, sir? I'm sorry to have to ask, but have you considered whether you would prefer cremation or burial?"

Two hours earlier, I was a father trying to figure out how we were going to manage with three kids in the house. Now I was faced with a completely different set of decisions. Buried or burned. These were really my options? These were the things I had to worry about now.

I know the chaplain was just doing his job, but I was disgusted by his blunt way of asking. Had I considered? In the last fifteen minutes, I had learned I would never hold my living, breathing child again. In what world would I have considered how I would like to dispose of his little body? I was incredulous. "It doesn't really matter now, does it? Do I have to make this decision right now, at this moment?" I asked.

He doubled down. "I'm sorry. I know this is difficult, but we need to notify the funeral home of your wishes." I couldn't stomach the idea of my baby boy being consumed by fire, and I knew Emily wouldn't be able to either.

"Buried," I answered, shaking my head in disgust as I re-entered the quiet room.

I didn't tell Emily about my decision. Family was starting to arrive, and my fire department family was already orchestrating ways to wrap their arms around us. I cannot speak highly enough of these men and women. One of the ER techs had asked earlier if we needed someone to get Caia from school, an offer I gratefully accepted. She soon arrived, but at only five-years-old, I don't believe she comprehended the gravity of what I said when I informed her of the death of her baby brother.

That was the worst conversation I have ever had. I explained it was okay to be sad and asked her if she knew what it meant to be dead. Surprisingly, she shook her head yes and said it was kind of like he would be asleep for a long time. That was as mature of an answer as I could have expected from her, and I decided to leave it at that. She didn't cry or react, but I sensed a personality change in her in the days following that told me that though she did not understand what was going on, she did understand it was bad and her family was heartbroken.

Emily had grown tired of the quiet room and simply wanted to leave. It was unclear to both of us what was expected of us, and after learning there was nothing further, I asked my best friend, Ryan, to run to our car to remove Brayden's car seat. I didn't want Emily to have to face that reminder, and frankly, I didn't want to either. I also asked him to go the house and pick up whatever toys he could find and place them in Brayden's room and shut the door. That door would remain shut for the next three months.

CHAPTER 6
BLOOD DOESN'T MAKE FAMILY

Today, Emily and I laid our son to rest with the support of the greatest group of men and women I have ever known. For every one of you who have called, messaged, offered your assistance in any way, offered your condolences, paid personal visits and cried with us, whatever the case may be, you have all been there for us and we could never thank you enough or repay you in a way that would be fitting. One of the things that you think about when you lose a child is all the things that they will never do, but when I saw the ladder arch, the helicopter flyover, the several apparatus' from various cities and municipalities, and the hundreds of you standing behind us to honor my son and crying with us, I know that my son went out with all the honor and respect that I believe he would have achieved in a lifetime, and that eases our pain just a little bit. Emily and I were dreading this day but to have you all there meant the world to us.

This evening, once the people went home and the house got quiet, we spent some time on the porch while Caia and Uncle Josh blew bubbles in the front yard, and we reflected on the many things that Brayden did that made us laugh. It felt good to think about him and smile. So, while this was a sad day for us and for many of you, we hope that you will remember him as he was in life and not as he was in death, because we know that our son is in heaven smiling, and sadness was impossible when Brayden was smiling.

*We would like to extend a personal thanks to **Ryan Gray** who has been with us from the moment we left the hospital to the time we left the service and beyond and who will be here in the next few coming days and for co-ordinating the service with the fire dept and various agencies to make all this special stuff as well as screening the calls that I just couldn't handle.*

*To **John Parrish**, who has been here bright and early cooking breakfast and doing dishes and at times just sitting quietly in the other room waiting for someone to ask something of him, and for purchasing a ceiling fan to replace one in our living room that has never worked(which was an extremely special gesture to my grieving wife, Brayden was obsessed with the rotating motion of ceiling fans.)*

To Britney and Chris Donivan, who have been here from the moment they found out and sitting up with us at night while we took turns in grief, and for running various errands and taking care of housekeeping and cooking.

To Captain Bostic for being there the moment I made the call and for orchestrating all the assistance with the FD that you have all been providing us to give us time to heal, and for just sitting with us and making us smile. You can't help but be distracted when Boz is around.

I wish that I could extend a personal thanks to each and every one of you, but this post would be miles long, so for any that were left out, we thank you from the bottom of our hearts. Many of you have said that you wish you could take our pain. Well, you have eased it quite a bit. You are all amazing.
-Chad Davis, Facebook, May 8, 2014

One thing that never ceases to amaze me is how the brotherhood pulls together in the times of tragedy. I can say with certainty that without these men and women, Emily and I would not have survived. This part is about the three days between the news and laying our son to rest, but at its heart, it is a testament to the strength one can draw from community, and the hearts and spirits and minds of these men and women who have dedicated their lives in service to others.

That dedication is even stronger when it is one of your own and is really an awesome and dumbfounding thing to witness. My grandfather remarked in awe of the love and support shown to us saying, "I've often worried about you down here all by yourself and away from the family, but after seeing this display of love, I know I don't have to worry anymore. You have a family here who takes care of you, in some ways, better than blood can." He could not have been more correct.

From the time we returned home, I cannot recall a time when there was not someone there with us. The fire department pulled together to not only ensure all of my shifts would be covered without me having to use leave time, but also to ensure Ryan could do the same so we would not be alone. Britney and Chris busied themselves balling melons and setting up charcuterie trays for the work parties and family arrivals.

I am not sure who started it, but a meal train was established. Huge meals arrived at twelve and five on the dot, and pretty soon, both of my refrigerators were overflowing with food, so I had to stop the train. I was fielding dozens of calls per hour, and while I was appreciative of the love and support being poured out on us, I was growing tired of accepting condolences and the "if there is any-thing you need, let me know" offers. I passed my phone off to Ryan, and he gave the scripted "as well as can be imagined" and "thank yous" for me.

If I needed to go somewhere, he drove me. If we needed something, he went out and got it or assigned someone else to the task. He was the man. I'm not even sure I could quantify everything he did because so much of it was behind the scenes. He also helped manage the funeral planning and acted as a go-between for Margie, my mother-in-law's best friend, who was picking caskets and arranging flowers. I am deeply grateful for Margie. We had barely spoken prior to this, but she saw a place she could help and jumped in. No parent should have to plan their child's funeral, and she wasn't going to allow us to.

Captain Parish, one of the most calming and pleasant people I have ever met but also a man that I had spent very little time with, spent countless hours on our couch in the front living room just reading the newspaper. He was quiet, but he was present and ready for any request. He arrived early, sometimes before we woke, and made breakfast, and then returned to his post on the couch to read the newspaper while everyone else ate. One afternoon, somebody mentioned it was hot, and he learned our ceiling fan was not working. He left without saying anything and returned with a brand new fan, and he and Boz installed it.

Boz was my first call after we learned of Brayden's death and was the cog that set this whole thing in motion. He was always present and remains so, even to this day, despite hundreds of miles between us. He paid for the entire funeral, and then was mad when he found out I knew it was him. That is just who he is.

The Portsmouth Sheriff, a man I didn't know, said that no Portsmouth Firefighter would bury his son without a personal escort from his men, and he personally led the detail of motorcycle mounted officers to escort us to the graveside. Other surrounding departments found ways to show support as well. The Chesapeake Fire Department backfilled Portsmouth stations so more of our firefighters could attend the service. The Suffolk Fire Department, who was initially tasked with saving Brayden, lined the road along the route to the graveside with engines pulled out and ladders raised, saluting as we drove by. Nightingale, the local air ambulance, did a "fly over" at the cemetery, a gesture that touched me deeply. It was clear the little man had made an impact in our community, and now our community was making an impact on us. I tear up reflecting on it even now.

I drew one other conclusion from this experience of community support. I cannot pretend to know why God allows bad things to happen to good people. In its purest form, it is a selfish question because it assumes the person asking is, in fact, a good person or that our goodness should somehow immunize us from facing hardships. We all face them at some point.

I recently witnessed a friend publicly thanking others for their prayers after her husband's biopsy returned benign. Another friend remarked, "Maybe next time you can ask him for me. I must be doing something wrong." This friend had fought through cancer, as well as other difficult trials, and I understood her anger and frustration, but on both occasions, she received the support of community in much the same way we did.

I think, sometimes, God uses these trials to wrap His love around us in the form of community. It is easy to be angry or to discount Him based on the trial, but when you reflect on this kind of love, the more powerful statement is seeing how you were carried through it. A "footprints in the sand" moment if you will. It is this community that has kept me going in this profession even when the days have been hard. One does not simply walk away from love like that.

Emily and I diverged in how we handled those first few days. For all intents and purposes, she entered into a catatonic state. Her eyes were always red, and her absent gaze rarely deviated from its fixed position. She barely spoke and used only one-word responses when she did. The only exception was her familiar recitation of, "He was my baby, my baby boy." She stopped eating on her own, and when pushed, she was resistant until she would capitulate and take in a single cookie and a sip of water.

I busied myself with entertaining guests and attempting to remain supportive of her. Our air conditioner broke, and I spent time outside with the guys trying to fix it. I loathed the sympathetic looks from those who arrived to offer their condolences and attempted to maintain a brave face when asked how we were holding up. "We're managing," I'd say, but we weren't. I didn't like to be alone. Those were the moments when my brave face strategy would collapse.

The morning of the funeral, I found myself in the shower staring at the door. I used to hang Brayden's kangaroo bouncer on the door frame while I showered, and he would get excited and bounce enthusiastically as I peeked around the corner at him in a rousing game of peek-a-boo. This time there was no laughter, no bouncing, no Brayden, and the wind escaped my lungs. I began sobbing uncontrollably and couldn't hold myself up. I slumped down into the shower and couldn't get up. Hearing me from downstairs, Emily burst through the doors and wrapped me in her arms. It seemed like no matter when one of us fell apart, the other seemed to be able to pull it together enough to lend strength. "No matter what, we will get through this together," we would repeat.

People remained in our home for a week, but slowly, there were fewer and fewer faces to distract me. Ryan had been away from his family for five days, maybe more, so I sent him home. It then dwindled to just my coworkers who would arrive for two to three hours, and then leave to give us our space. I think Emily preferred to be alone, but our home was full of reminders a baby had once lived there. A spit-up stain on the carpet, a pacifier that had been lost in the sofa. These reminders stirred my anger, and Emily remained stagnant in her grief process. I was growing frustrated.

Six days after Brayden's death, Mother's Day arrived, and I wished her a Happy Mother's Day. She grew angry and told me not to say that to her because she wasn't a mother anymore. I tried to comfort her with reassurance that she was a mother to Caia, and she would always be Brayden's mom, but she retorted "Caia has a mom, and my baby is dead." I buried her Mother's Day card in the bottom of my sock drawer and forgot about it until we moved years later.

We had a vacation planned to Florida for my friend Dustin's wedding on

May 13th. I was supposed to be the best man in his wedding, but I cancelled when Brayden died, thinking there was no way that we would be in any condition to go. However, as I rolled the idea over in my mind, I saw an opportunity to escape the quiet, haunting walls of our home where my anger was beginning to build and go be around happy people on a happy occasion. Emily was reluctant, saying, "Don't you think we'll be complete downers?"

I wasn't sure, so I relayed her concerns to Dustin and Stacie, but like the good people they are, they reiterated their desire to have us there. So we packed our bags, cancelled the meal train, and put Virginia in the rearview mirror. It was a welcome distraction to see my childhood best friend and his new wife and partake in their happiness, but seven days later, reality struck when we had to return home.

The miles I had placed between us and our reality were only temporary and dwindled far too quickly, but the hours passed slowly and gave me plenty of time to reflect on the hell we were returning to. With each passing mile marker, the lump in my throat swelled, and I dreaded crossing the threshold into our home, absent one member. The air was stale with the sorrows of the previous week, and this time, there were no visitors, food, or other distractions to keep our minds occupied. The ordeal had ended for the community, who had returned to the normalcy of their everyday lives. As the country singer, Tracy Lawrence, so eloquently sang, "Time marches on." This was the first time we realized that though the world had moved on, we would continue to carry the same gut-wrenching pain that began only three weeks prior. It was us and four walls.

On May 21, 2014, the world's largest rubber duck, created by Dutch artist Florentijn Hofman, docked in a harbor in Norfolk. The duck was said to possess healing properties and could relieve the tensions of the world. In reality, the artist was talking about bringing the world together through the oddity of having a giant, yellow duck parked alongside aircraft carriers and cruise ships, but we needed the healing, and happiness was in short supply, so we figured it was worth a shot. We visited, took some pictures of us smiling in front of it, posted them on social media to prove to the world we were doing fine, and marveled at a big duck in the water.

I remember worrying what people would think if they saw us smiling. Was two and a half weeks long enough to wait before reintroducing the smile? This was a common theme in those first few months. I often wondered if I was acting appropriately. Was I sad enough? Was I too sad? I'm not sure why it mattered. I remember feeling guilt for even partaking in such a trivial event. Who goes to such a ridiculous display less than three weeks after the death of their child?

These photos popped up in my Facebook Memories recently, and in retrospect, those concerns were a non-factor because the expressions we wore were clearly hollow. My smile was subdued, almost non-existent, and did nothing to hide the pain we were experiencing. Emily's seemed marginally more genuine, but the sunglasses she wore covered her bloodshot eyes. Nonetheless, the duck had succeeded in giving us a brief respite from the hollowness we felt, and it was the first time I had seen Emily smile since the morning of May 5th, so I counted it as a win.

The so-called healing properties of the duck were short-lived. The silence reminded us constantly of what we had lost. We weren't eating. Our sleep schedules became more intermittent, and at times, we would wake up in the middle of the night and just wander the house. I sometimes walked to his room, desiring to be close to some piece of him, only to stop and stare at the closed door, weighing the consequences of opening it. The anger would well up in my throat, and I would choke it down and return to bed for another few minutes of broken sleep.

They say idle hands make Devil's work, and I can say with certainty that Satan was using these moments to break us. I needed to start moving and return to some semblance of normalcy. I resented her inability to do so. "No matter what, we will get through this together," I repeated to myself, not sure that I believed it. It was not long before I had had enough of the stalemate. We weren't living, we were just existing. I wanted to get back to work, and I told Emily we needed to just keep putting one foot in front of the other. "One second, one minute, one step at a time" became my mantra, but she seemed unconvinced.

Privately, I messaged Ryan and said, "I wish she would get up, all she does is sleep now." He urged me to remain supportive. The next day, Emily popped out of bed, showered, and declared her intent to return to work as well. I didn't understand her change of heart, but I was grateful for it. It was only recently I learned that through the magic of interconnected Apple devices, she had seen that message on the computer and felt like she was letting me down. I wish I had never said it.

After twenty-one days of bereavement, we both went back to work. Our experiences were vastly different. I returned to the same family that had carried us through the funeral while Emily returned to the hospital. Few of her co-workers were sympathetic. There was no attempt to protect her, and one nurse even remarked,

"We're going to give you all the pediatric patients to help you get over it." Another told her she would never make it as a nurse now. Somehow, she endured, although those cold statements were the catalysts leading to the path she would ultimately take. I was not so durable.

On my second night back to work, we were dispatched to a vehicle accident. The patient, a drunk driver, was belligerent and testing my patience. I told her to sit down and shut her mouth. "You should be nicer! People who have been in car accidents aren't very nice people and you should know that!" she slurred. I lost it. For me, it was personal for the first time in my career. I truly believe I would have killed her if not for the intervention of my coworkers.

"People who have lost kids aren't very nice either, but you don't see me in here acting like an asshole!" I screamed in her face.

"Out! Get out!" the other paramedic said as she grabbed me and pushed me through the back doors. "Take him," she told my crew before shutting the door behind me.

I was sent back to the station where I had a late-night meeting with my captain. He sent me home and referred me to the employee assistance program, probably as much to save my job as to get me the help I had been unaware I needed. It was clear to all involved I was not in the mental state yet to endure the stresses of sleepless nights and abusive patients.

CHAPTER 7

GOD SHOWS UP

Two days after I was sent home, I sat in a Chick-Fil-A for lunch, and the song "Mighty to Save" played over the intercom. I had grown up in the church but had long been questioning of God's existence or role in our lives. I was somewhere between agnostic and atheistic. I had not thought about God since Brayden's death, but on this day, the song angered me, and I began to argue with a being I wasn't sure I believed in. If you have not heard the song, the chorus goes like this:

Savior

He can move the mountains

My God is Mighty to save

He is Mighty to save

Forever

Author of salvation

He rose and conquered the grave

Jesus conquered the grave

I became infuriated and tears began to well up in my eyes. I stood up, threw my uneaten food in the garbage, and stormed out to my truck where I slammed my hand into the steering wheel. "If you're so mighty, why couldn't you save my son?" I screamed at the windshield. I slammed the gearshift into drive and squealed tires out of the parking lot. I wasn't thirty seconds down the road before I was deafened and disoriented by a voice—or a thought—I can't explain. It had an assertive commanding tone, but I did not feel scolded.

"DO YOU REALLY BELIEVE THAT I AM SMALLER THAN THE GRAVE?" It thundered.

I became dizzy and nauseated and had to pull over into the parking lot of an abandoned gas station where I wept until my senses returned. I felt naked and ashamed, stripped of the walls I had built up between myself and God over the years. I believed I had experienced the voice of God, but was also concerned I was maybe a little crazy. I didn't tell anyone about the experience initially, but on the second session with the therapist, I told him I was concerned I was hearing voices.

I relayed my experience, and he asked if I had heard the voice since then. "No," I replied. The corners of his mouth turned up. He put his notepad down, folded his hands, and leaned back in his chair. He sat quietly for a moment before he spoke.

"Often in The Bible, when Jesus was confronted with a question of faith, he responded with a question in much the same way your question was answered with a question. When Jesus was confronted with the death of Lazarus, The Bible says that He wept. Jesus knew the miracle that He was about to perform, but it says that He wept anyway. Why do you suppose that is?"

I said nothing.

He continued. "I believe that this shows that He is empathetic toward what we are going through. I don't think that it is outside the realm of possibility that God spoke to you to let you know that He cares about what you are going through."

I pondered that for a moment. "But God hasn't spoken to people directly since the Old Testament. Why would He speak to me now?" I asked.

"God may not speak in the linguistic ways that people necessarily inter-pret as speech, but the world is full of stories of God speaking in various ways. You are admittedly an atheist. Maybe the only way God felt he could get through to you was to speak directly to your heart."

I was stunned this therapist was not prescribing medication for schizo-phrenia. I asked about his background to find out he had roots in the Church of God, a sect of the Pentecostal denomination, and the same denomination I had grown up in. He was the first person I had encountered from the Church of God in several years, and I think that of all the therapists I could have been assigned, it was not a coincidence I was assigned to him.

While I pondered renewing my faith, Emily found solace in staying busy and immersed herself in her work. She worked night and day it seemed, and when she wasn't working, she was sleeping. She added a second job and then a bachelor's degree to her resume, but that wasn't enough. She was dealing with her pain by not dealing with it all and was fast becoming burnt out. She dreaded every shift, felt like an outsider, and perceived a lack of empathy in her coworkers, often reciting the phrase, "Nurses eat their own."

She grew tired of bedside nursing, so she embarked on a mission to obtain her master's degree so she could move into nursing education. She conquered this achievement in just sixteen months, and then took a job teaching nursing at a local college, promising that she was done. However, to be done meant she would have to face her grief. She was unhappy at that college and transitioned to another one, but this school required her to obtain a Doctoral degree.

In spite of my insistence on slowing down, she added a doctoral program and two more jobs to her schedule. Her thesis was a referendum on her experiences as a bereaved mother and bedside nurse and stemmed from the comments made upon her return to work. "We're going to give you all the pediatric patients so you can get over it." Seeing the stark contrast between the support I received and the general lack of empathy she was shown day after day, nurse after nurse, she concluded nurses generally lack the emotional intelligence to understand how their words and actions are perceived by others. She also determined ER nurses lack a sense of empathy and were jaded, particularly in busy hospitals, and she set out to change it. Prior studies had indicated emotional intelligence was not a teachable skill, but her research and conclusions determined it could in fact be taught and should begin in the classroom before a nurse ever touches a patient by setting this expectation from the outset.

In addition to drowning herself in her work and school, she was also nurturing a life inside of her. We would be lying if we said we did not expect a miscarriage. Brayden was a difficult pregnancy that followed multiple miscarriages and was only carried to term with the aid of progesterone suppositories and daily blood thinner injections. It seemed impossible this baby would survive to term with the stresses and emotional turmoil she was suffering.

Our fears were realized in a Red Lobster one afternoon after she went to the bathroom to find she had begun bleeding. We called the obstetrician to see if the pregnancy could be salvaged, but to our dismay, the heartbeat persisted, and the bleeding resolved. Day after day, we waited for the other shoe to drop, but it didn't. The baby inside her became her reason to keep going. The longer the pregnancy continued, the more I feared that losing him would destroy her fragile emotional state, but on December 2, 2014, we welcomed baby Maddox into the world.

Parenting a newborn is hard. Parenting a newborn seven months after losing a child to Sudden Infant Death Syndrome (SIDS) is nothing short of Hell. I am not sure I slept more than an hour at a time for the first six months of his life. I spent countless nights standing over the crib, determined not to let death take another one. To make matters worse, we had invested in a sleep apnea alarm to place under his mattress that would alert us if he stopped breathing. We quickly learned babies stop breathing *a lot*, and he would sometimes move off the sensor pad entirely. When the alarm went off, we would run to his room only to find he was fine.

After six months of this, I was exhausted and basically decided if it was going to happen, there would be nothing I could do to stop it. We disconnected the alarm, and I stopped getting up as often, but I continued to roll over and watch him on the camera. Boys between four and eight months of age are at higher risk for SIDS, so I relaxed a bit after the eight-month mark. At a year, I held an internal celebration and thanked God we had made it. Emily envisioned our two boys growing up together, and we had discussions about having another child, but after the year of lost sleep, worry, and constant fear, I could not bring myself to do it again.

That first year was tough on the home front, but professionally, it was a nightmare. After a couple months away from the department, I was nervous to go back. The pain was still raw, and I constantly worried I would be a shell of what I was before. I had no idea how I would react to death, long sleepless nights, stressful situations, child abuse, rape, neglect, or the event I feared the most, the death of a child. I worried I would freeze under pressure and be unable to perform when it mattered. I constantly ran scenarios in my head, rehearsed procedures, and practiced speaking and giving direction, step by step, second by second, and then I would do it all over again.

I worried others would coddle me and attempt to shield me from the event or would look to me for direction and would find none. Nobody wants to be the weak link. Oddly, but perhaps not accidentally, I went several years without having another pediatric cardiac arrest. Thank God for small mercies, but there had been a definite change in my outlook. I became less tolerant of petty problems. I found it difficult to empathize with suicidal patients or to express sympathy to those who had just lost a parent or a grandparent. It just didn't feel like it compared to my own loss, and I began to feel guilty for diminishing the pain of others.

I changed my bad news delivery methods as well. Reflecting on my own experience, I retired the euphemisms and became brutally and robotically blunt. "I'm sorry, but she's dead," and then I would walk away and leave the emotional support to someone else. I didn't feel the same enthusiasm for the "good calls," and I implemented a personal "one person in" policy on the more gruesome scenes to reduce exposure to the mental trauma for as many people as possible, unless more assistance was absolutely necessary. I also didn't tolerate sleep deprivation as well anymore and became more irritable at home. I knew I had a difficult decision to make. My time in Portsmouth was coming to an end. I either needed a change of scenery, or I needed to end my career.

At about the time I began to question my future, an opportunity presented itself with a more rural department with a much lower call volume. They had recently hired a former Portsmouth Battalion Chief with whom I already had a well-established relationship as their Chief. He had encouraged me to go to paramedic school earlier in my career. It seemed like the right fit at the right time, and I applied and was offered an interview.

I prepared in the way I always prepare. I've been through these interviews before. They're all pretty much the same, so I wasn't shocked when the standard questions popped up. "Tell me about a time where you encountered conflict and how you dealt with it." "What would you say is your greatest strength? Weakness? How do you handle that weakness?"

The weakness question is my secret weapon. I don't want to give the cliché answer, "Perfection. I'm too perfect." I would never hire anybody that told me that, so I have a patent on my own answer. "When faced with difficult decisions, I have a tendency to become introspective. This can seem like I'm uncertain or indecisive, but in my head, I'm just thinking through the problem and planning my next move. I'm aware of this and force myself to think out loud. This allows newer providers to have a front row seat to my thought process and gives more senior providers the opportunity to weigh in and give their opinion. In this way, it makes everyone better."

I could see the HR manager was impressed. "That's a really good answer," she told me as she wrote it down. I knew I was nailing this. And then I met a new friend, PTSD. "Tell me about an emotional call you've had."

That one caught me like lace on a rusty nail. I hesitated. "I…uh, I had a two-year old… that I, uh…she, um…." I could feel the lump in my throat swelling up again, and my voice began to break. I was speaking about a pediatric cardiac arrest from several years prior, but in my head, now only one year removed from the death of my son, I was fully back in the hospital room watching Brayden's unsupported head falling back. In front of the HR manager, a fire department captain, and my prospective fire chief, I experienced my first PTSD sneak attack.

As the tears began to flow, I could feel the tension in the room rising, and I knew I needed to move on and get out of this question. "She, uh…went into cardiac arrest, and we, uh…we just worked her." They were as happy to write down the answer and move on as I was. Nobody complimented my response. What are the chances that question has been removed? I left feeling dejected.

"How'd it go?" Emily asked.

"Terrible. I cried in my interview. Guess I won't be getting that job."

I was wrong. On June 1, 2015, I left Portsmouth and began a new chapter. It was not without drawbacks though. To leave Portsmouth meant to leave a supportive fire department family who knew my story and were attentive and understanding of my bad days. I am certain my career would not have survived another year if not for having had these men and women to lean on. I felt guilty for turning my back on them, but I knew I had to do something to save my career and mental health.

It also meant the majority of my transports would be to the hospital where Brayden had been transported. I worried that every time I placed a patient in that room, I would relive the experiences surrounding his death. Those worries were well founded, and I did experience some of that, but the trade-off for sleeping at night and handling a different type of clientele far removed from the hood was worth the change—at least for a while. It also meant I would be breaking up with my personal identity. I would no longer be a firefighter except in title. My primary job was as a paramedic and a firefighter only in the absence of volunteers. That was a tough pill to swallow, but I quickly got used to my new role.

I have formed tight bonds with my partners over the years, but I never again experienced the sort of family closeness I left behind in Portsmouth. I liken it to when you leave your parents' home for the first time, and from then on, nowhere else really feels like home. I realize now those relationships were formed through the process of maturation from being the "new guy" to becoming a seasoned vet. They were born out of a sense of admiration and respect for veteran knowledge I did not yet possess and their willingness to bring me along until I finally measured up to their standards, and in turn, my willingness to do the same for the next guy. They grew out of years of handling family problems within the family and supporting each other as we endured life's hardships, complexities, and celebrated the little victories together.

I realized it would be nearly impossible to ever find that again. I also learned that I divide my life into two halves—the half before Brayden, and the half that came after his passing. Connecting with people since his passing has been a gargantuan challenge. It feels impossible to be fully myself with part of me missing and niceties just feel so hollow. I feel obligated to withhold that part of my story because it makes people uncomfortable. Those who I do share it with tend to avoid the subject afterwards, and it makes me distance myself and resent them. It is hard to have friends when you begin on such an unsteady platform. The loneliness runs deep.

In 2018, Emily was offered a job teaching at a college in Indiana. Though the slower pace of life I had gained as a country medic had helped, professionally I was stagnant, so there was really no reason to stay. We both agreed breaking ties with the geography would be beneficial to our healing. It was difficult passing the cemetery. At first, we stopped often, but slowly, we began to visit less and less. The less we stopped, the guiltier we felt. The guiltier we felt, the more we stopped, and with each stop, the wound reopened, and the cycle repeated. We constantly had to remind ourselves the boy we loved was not there anyway.

On cool, sunny days, flashbacks of the race to the hospital surfaced, and I could still look over and see the ghosts of drivers past cursing my lack of consideration for others on the road as I desperately tried to get to my son, dead in his hospital bed. Our home, once lively with the energy of a six-month-old who had just figured out how to crawl, remained a grim reminder of what we had lost, and we didn't want to look at it anymore. We felt we had given it enough time that we weren't being rash, so we just left. There was no real discussion, no pomp and circumstance, and very little planning. In late September, we went to see a Cubs game, stopping in Indiana on the way to visit Dustin and Stacie, and by December, we were living in Indiana. It was as if we had both been feeling a magnetic pull and only needed the other to vocalize it to affirm the notion.

However, I had one more thing to do. Four years after the worst day of my life, with three shifts left at my job, the moment I feared most finally happened. Dispatched to a patient with breathing difficulty at a local doctor's office, I arrived to find a baby boy sucking in his last breath. We snatched him up, ran out to the ambulance, and got to work. I pushed air into his lungs with a bag valve mask and administered lifesaving drugs to open his airways. We were making progress, and his heart rate was maintaining.

I attempted to place a tube into his throat, but his jaw clenched, and he began to seize. I administered valium to stop the seizure and decided to stop at a closer hospital to stabilize him before proceeding to a children's hospital. I reassured the mother things were going well and expressed cautious optimism for a good outcome if things continued to progress as they were.

When we arrived, I straddled the head of the stretcher with the baby between my legs, and my crew pushed us in while I continued to breathe for him. Once the baby was safely under the care of the physician. I retreated to the ambulance as the dam holding back twenty minutes of tension and stress finally gave way. I was okay though, if not ecstatic, that I had performed when I needed to and had been able to save this moment for after the call. A few days later, I learned the baby had been weaned from the ventilator and was playing in the hospital as if nothing had happened. This was a rare win on a dynamic, evolving call, and it was on the patient I most dreaded. But for me, this win was bigger. It was confirmation I was not yet done.

CHAPTER 8

THE GOOD TIMES

It's a game you're not even aware you're playing, a dance on a fence rail that sometimes leaves you on the wrong side of burnout. There's a lot of bad in our world, and it's easy to believe our fate is bleak, destined to end up lying in our own feces in a disgusting nursing home, being fed through a tube. Perhaps we will die tragically in a car accident, or our memory will fail, and we won't remember the names of our children or spouse, living out our days scared of everything and wondering who the stranger is that talks to us like we should know them. That's the world we dwell in, so it's easy to forget the vast majority of people die comfortably in their beds and never suffer.

We feel the weight of the tragedies and the suffering, of the neglected children, the addicted, the mentally broken, and the relentless onslaught of the absolute nonsense calls. If this was all our world consisted of, we wouldn't last five years in this career, but it's not. Amidst the chaos, tragedy, horror, unspeakable misery, and the ridiculous, there is occasionally a call where we're able to do some good. They're few and far between, but when we get one, it brings a sense of pride and accomplishment that keeps us going until the next one comes.

Sometimes, you can find some tidbit of humor in a call that will make you laugh and provide entertainment with your guys back at the station. If you look carefully, you can find that in most calls. These stories are told through generations of new firefighters and paramedics and are often the glue that binds this generation to the next. These are the stories that allow firefighters to visit a station long after they retire and to pick up as if they've known each other forever, because in a sense, they have. These are the calls that keep us going and pull us back from the desire to just walk away. Some days are good days.

Zombies Among Us

"I don't know anything about him. He's not my patient. He just got here yesterday. I just came on shift," the nurse rattled off, the nursing home superfecta. These are a series of excuses for why the nursing home nurse can't tell us anything about the patient. We hear them anytime we walk into a nursing home and have grown accustomed to leaving without any real information about the patients. As a matter of fact, we take bets on which one it will be, but tonight, we were all wrong and all right. This nurse used them all. A grand slam! I was impressed.

I arrived at the room to find a CNA performing CPR on the patient. This was a surprise since we were told this call was for a diabetic. We had walked all the way from the front entry way with a nurse giving us reasons she didn't know anything about this patient, and through the *entire* journey, nobody said anything about a cardiac arrest. That's par for the course though, and I was prepared.

Over the years, I've learned to bring all the equipment when entering a nursing home because their sense of serious is not the same as ours. On airway was an LPN, ventilating the patient with a bag valve mask. Again, I was impressed. This must have been the dream team. Usually, they just put an oxygen mask on the patient, which is great for the living, but for everyone else, it doesn't do any good if they can't breathe the oxygen being supplied. Upon closer examination, I realized she was holding the mask upside down. I took the BVM from her, turned the mask over, and handed it back. "Try it that way," I said politely.

She laughed and said, "I was wondering why all the air was coming out the sides!"

We got down to business. Obviously the patient was in cardiac arrest. "How long has he been down?" I asked.

"We found him like this about ten minutes ago. We just talked to him earlier, and he was doing fine," she informed me.

The standard answer again. It's like they have a script they read from. I checked for a pulse and found none. "Does he have any advanced directives?" I asked. They stared at me blankly. I rephrased. "A DNR." Again, blank stares.

Right on cue, the "I don't know him" nurse appeared again with the paperwork, and then quickly disappeared again to do whatever it is they do when they disappear. I shook my head in disbelief and turned my attention to the packet of paperwork. It probably had more information than she did anyway.

Shuffling through it, I found the yellow paper with the red letters and stop sign at the top that I was looking for. This document outlined the patient's wishes not to be resuscitated when the time came. I confirmed the patient's signature and ensured it had been signed by the doctor. It all checked out. This was all I needed. "You can stop," I told them. "Time of death, 2058."

The nurses cleared the room and went back to their business. We covered the patient and made the body presentable for any family that wished to visit before the funeral home arrived and stepped out of the room to complete the paperwork. Boz and I stood outside of the doorway filling in the blanks when something in the room caught my eye. The dead man's leg jumped up into the air. My heart dropped into my stomach. My biggest fear as a paramedic had been to pronounce someone dead who was not actually dead, but I was *certain* I had felt no pulse. "Oh, no," I said to Boz.

"What?" he asked.

"He *moved*." I started back into the room, but Boz grabbed me and pulled me back.

"Don't you go back in there. Not yet. Are you sure he moved?"

I pondered for a moment. Maybe he was right. Maybe my mind was playing tricks on me. Maybe I didn't see what I thought I saw. Maybe it was just a shadow from a passing vehicle. I reluctantly accepted that theory but continued to watch nervously. Boz was now on alert, too.

After a few moments, the leg kicked up into the air again. It wasn't my imagination after all. This time we had both seen it and couldn't deny it. We approached cautiously, half expecting the dead man to spring from his bed and chase us from the room, but he did no such thing. He just laid there as peacefully as I had left him. I pressed my fingers into his carotid artery and again felt nothing. He had no pulse. I checked his pulse at the groin as well and found nothing there either. Boz checked behind me and agreed.

As we stood there trying to figure out what was going on, the leg jumped into the air again, and we both jumped backwards. This time I had seen the muscles in his neck contract and his arms went rigid in synchrony with the zombie leg. It occurred to me this was something I had seen before, but never without action from my own hand. I pulled back his gown and on his right upper chest, found a small square pushing up from beneath the skin. I returned to the patient's chart and confirmed my suspicion. There, in the history, I found it. "Automatic Internal Cardiac Defibrillator."

This is a device that had been installed into his chest designed to shock him whenever he was in the lethal arrhythmias of Ventricular Tachycardia or Ventricular Fibrillation. I was relieved my fear of prematurely declaring someone dead had not transpired. I had been correct. He didn't have a pulse, but the little device was trying to bring one back. We waited awhile to see if it worked, but this patient's heart was done. Nature took its course, and the jumping stopped after a few more frightening jolts.

Back at the station, the captain retold the story of the zombie and how the color drained from my face. "He looked like he had seen a ghost!"

I guess I kind of had. Never again did I pronounce someone dead without some ribbing and a friendly reminder of this incident. "Are you sure?"

Is He Gone?

"Start triaging. There are bodies everywhere." I had arrived onto a bloody gang battleground, and tonight, there didn't seem to be any winners. There never are when it comes to senseless killing. I had been assigned to triage the sector beneath a solitary oak tree where most of the carnage seemed to have occurred. The EMS supervisor was checking the rest of the bodies scattered around the scene.

As I approached the tree, I saw a mass of people stacked one on top of another and set to work. Pulling the top man off the pile, I checked his pulse and found nothing. The hole in his head explained the lack of pulse, and I declared him a black tag, the designation of the deceased in a mass casualty incident. I pulled the second man off and placed him next to the first man. I lifted his shirt to find multiple gunshot wounds through his torso, and again, no pulse. My second black tag.

I repeated this process twice more and began to realize this was a fruitless endeavor. These men were all dead. Returning to the final man, lying lifeless at the bottom of the pile, I went through the motions once more. He laid unmoving, the glaze of a dead man filling his eyes. I surveyed him from a distance and noted holes through both cheeks, a through and through gunshot wound. I pulled him up by the shirt collar to be dragged over and laid next to his buddies, but suddenly his limp body went rigid, and he grabbed my arms. "Is he gone?" screamed the corpse. I fell backwards.

"What the fuck?" I responded in kind.

"I was playing dead," he said. "He shot me first, and I just fell down and stopped moving! I turned my head at the last minute and saw him coming, and he shot me through the cheek, so I fell down and pretended to be dead, but I guess they didn't, and they just fell on top of me. I was too scared to move!"

His last second turn had saved his life, allowing the bullet intended for the back of his head to pass relatively harmlessly through the cheeks.

Later, back at the station, my partner couldn't get the words out through his laughter as he reenacted my fall backwards. "Is he…is he…is he *gone*?" he said through wheezy laughter with tears in his eyes.

Hot Dog

I was on the third engine to arrive on the scene of a dryer fire, which essentially meant I had nothing to do. The first engine was inside making the fire attack. The second engine had wrapped the hydrant and was laying out the water supply. The ladder was conducting a search for any victims and opening windows to remove the smoke from the house. The rescue truck was assigned to the rapid intervention team, which was to be activated if a firefighter went down, and then there was me, the third engine, the reserve engine. My job was to do whatever I was told to do, but for the moment, there was nothing to do, so I just watched. The radio came to life.

"Primary search all clear. We're exiting the structure." The ladder crew exited, but the chief had just received a report there were still family pets inside.

"Ladder Ten, change your air bottles and go look for the animals."

A few moments later, they reentered the house, and it wasn't long before the radio crackled again. "We've located the dog. We're coming out." A firefighter exited the front door with a smoked Schnauzer and dumped him on the lawn in front of me. The dog had succumbed to the fumes and was hanging on to life by a thread and a prayer, barely breathing.

We applied a puppy oxygen mask and rapped on his rib cage, hoping to stimulate him to breathe. I am no veterinarian. I had never treated a dog before, but Captain Boz hunts with dogs. He has had dogs wounded by bears or other wild animals before and had to treat them. He pulled out an IV catheter and searched for a vein in the dog's leg. Somehow, he was successful, and we hung a bag of IV fluids, uncertain as to whether this was appropriate care for a dog. We were treating this little dog as if it were a human, and even tiny humans aren't treated the same as big humans.

With each passing moment, the dog's breathing grew faster and stronger, but he remained unmoving. Finally, he fought to lift his head and kicked his legs as if he were a newborn fawn struggling to stand for the first time, but also like a fawn, had no coordination and fell flat again, having overexerted himself for the moment. "So, um. Now what?" I asked.

Captain Boz pulled out his phone and tracked down a twenty-four-hour emergency animal hospital, but we had a new problem. How would we get it there? Could we take an ambulance? No. Ambulances are for people, and if someone who needed an ambulance called and found out the closest one was transporting a dog, there would be no answering for that, especially if the person died. Boz made the decision that the best way to get it there was to take the EMS supervisor's vehicle and have me ride in the back with the dog.

We rode emergently to the animal hospital, and slowly but surely, the little Schnauzer gained strength, and his breathing began to relax. He finally sat up and began to lick my hand, seemingly content that we were the good guys, and his ordeal was over. He made no effort to leave my lap. I had a new best friend. By the time we arrived, the little dog was fully alert, and I passed the story on to the vet who seemed impressed we had made the efforts we had. They agreed to hold him overnight, and I later learned the little guy had survived. This was one of the good days.

A New Record

As the saying goes, there's two things firefighters hate; change and the way things are. In the previous week, we had been inundated with a whole lot of change in the medical world as our leadership began to integrate the new buzzword "evidence-based practice" into our treatment protocols. That is to say, we were changing the way we did things.

For a half a century, we had operated in a manner that was, essentially, because it made sense to us. There were few studies and little evidence behind the protocols we followed, but as EMS turned to science to improve prehospital patient outcomes, some of those methods had proven to be less effective than once thought. One of the greatest areas of change was in the field of cardiology. The algorithm had been rather simple since the early days of EMS. For any complaint of chest pain, the patient was placed on the monitor to assess their heart rhythm and ensure they were not in any lethal arrhythmias that could be remedied. We then administered aspirin to stop any further clots from forming, gave a sublingual, or "under the tongue," nitroglycerine to dilate the arteries in the heart, and drove really fast. Our goal had always been to get them to the ER where the doctors could work their medical magic.

This week, our administration had issued new heart monitors and modems to each ambulance. We were now expected to obtain a twelve lead EKG, which gives a complete picture of the electrical activity in the heart and could indicate the markers of a heart attack. In addition, we could now transmit this information to the hospital, which gave them a printout of what we were looking at in the field before we ever arrived at the hospital. In turn, they could activate the cardiac catheterization lab, which is definitive treatment to stop and reverse a heart attack. The goal was to reduce the amount of time sitting in the ER and reach the cath lab more quickly. Time is muscle, and muscle is life.

Immediately, the changes were met with resistance from the old timers. "By the time we sit on scene and get all this stuff, the patient is going to be dead! What happened to the good ol' days when we just threw them in the back of the hearse and hauled ass?" This argument was repeated ad nauseum throughout the week, but I was essentially a brand-new paramedic, and I didn't know enough to have an opinion on this just yet. I was kind of intrigued with the new process and excited to be given an expanded role. I was willing to give it a shot, and in short order, I was going to get my chance.

At lunch time, I had just bit into my grilled chicken sandwich when the station tones alerted me to a patient having chest pain. I groaned, put my sandwich down, and headed out the door. When I arrived, I found a man in his forties with the classic textbook presentation of a person having a heart attack. He was gray, or "ashen" in medical speak, sweaty, and clutching his chest. I needed no further assessment to determine it was time to go.

We gathered the patient, placed him on the stretcher and headed to the truck where I was waiting with the twelve lead cables and an IV. I obtained the EKG and the printout read ***MEETS STEMI CRITERIA***. This means the patient is having an ST Elevation Myocardial Infarction, fancy phraseology for "heart attack," and confirmed my suspicion. I hit the transmit button and sent the tracing to the doctor at the other end. With just six minutes to the hospital, I told my partner to drive, and I would do everything else in transit.

I gave the patient the aspirin and got on the radio with the hospital, relaying to them I was transporting a STEMI patient, and they told me to hold for physician review. After a few moments, the nurse returned to the radio. "Per the doctor, proceed directly to the cath lab." I returned to the patient and inserted an IV line in each arm and gave him the nitroglycerine. Upon arrival through the ER doors, I was greeted by a waiting ER tech who led me to the cath lab. There, I found the surgical team scrubbed and waiting. We pulled the patient to the table, and with our job completed, left the room.

However, I lingered in the observation room to watch the procedure. As they pushed the dye into the IV, I watched the heart vessels fill with the black substance and then drain over and over again. "There it is," said the radiologist, pointing to an area on the screen where the artery ended abruptly, revealing the location of the occluded vessel. "A complete blockage of the left anterior descending artery," he said.

"The *widow maker*," I marveled. "Fascinating."

With the blockage located, the surgeon advanced the tiny wire up through an artery in the patient's arm and into the heart, where he expanded the stent. A second injection of contrast dye was administered, and this time, the second half of the artery came alive with each pulsation.

"Fascinating," I repeated.

A few days later, my supervisor called me. "You know that STEMI patient you had the other day? He had a 'call to catheterization' time of thirty-nine minutes."

"Okay?" I asked. "Is that good?"

"Uh—yeah!" he exclaimed. "From the time the call came in, to the time the stint was placed, it was thirty-nine minutes. That's the fastest ever recorded in the state of Virginia!"

I received a meritorious conduct award for my efforts and became a diehard believer in the new protocols. I wasn't the only one. Over the next few weeks, the grumbling died down, and I noticed a few of those old timers taking the time to obtain those twelve leads they were so resistant to. Maybe you can teach an old dog new tricks.

The Tale of the Poo

The funny thing about the good times is they are often so damned miserable in the moment. Lift assists are the bread and butter of the fire service. There is a whole industry built around equipment intended for moving obese people around. From the floor to the bed, from the bed to the stretcher, from the stretcher to the ambulance, winches and ramps, and we had it all because so many in our response area suffered from morbid obesity.

Today we were dispatched to a familiar address we had been to many times but had never once transported the lady. She usually just needed a little help and did not abuse the system. She was a large woman, confined to the house for over a year simply because she would not fit through the door. As we arrived, we found her husband mounted on his throne atop the porch. He drew a drag from his cigarette and blew the smoke in our faces as he nonchalantly explained she was lying on the floor. "You'll find her," he said.

We entered the home and located her; larger than the last time we had seen her. If the obesity wasn't enough, she was wet, naked, and covered in feces. With people this large, there is nothing solid to grab. Up close and personal with multiple people is the name of this game, and the wetness, nudity, and defecation had complicated that matter. We determined it would be best to roll her onto the tarp, affectionately named the "Mega Mover," and lift her onto the stretcher with as many hands as we could get. However, she threw us a curveball when she told us she didn't want to go to the hospital. She just wanted help up. Ghastly looks swept over the entire crew as we all came to the same realization at the exact same moment. She had to be cleaned up.

We don't wipe butts. It's one of the unwritten rules of the fire service, but somebody *should* write it because we adhere to this policy as if God Himself engraved it in stone atop Mount Sinai. It's why we don't become nurses. Nurses wipe a lot of butts, God love 'em.

Captain Boz asked the question plaguing all our minds. "Once you get up, how are you going to clean yourself up? You can't reach back there."

She paused. "I'll get my husband to do it," she replied.

We all let out a collective sigh of relief. Satisfied with that answer, Captain Boz returned to the porch to suggest to the husband he clean her up before we moved her so she wouldn't have to get up again.

"I can't clean her up," he replied. "I'll get sick."

"You're kiddin,'" Boz said.

"Nope," said the man.

Disgusted, Boz returned to the house to think things over once more. After surveying the mess, he made a decision. Remember rule one? When in doubt, do what is right. "Go get some towels out of the medic," he ordered. "You don't have to help, but I'm going to clean her up."

It was the most "Boz" order imaginable. Never ask anything of your crew that you are not willing to do yourself, and when in doubt, do what is right. Ryan and I went to the ambulance and returned with every towel we could muster. Handing them to Boz, we retreated from the stench to the safety of the porch, leaving Boz alone with the regrets of his decisions.

For a moment, we leaned over the rail in silence as our minds raced. It's engraved in stone, man. If we wiped one butt, we'd have to wipe them all, and I wasn't ready to take on that kind of commitment. I had, like, twenty-five years left. Boz would only have to live with the consequences of this decision for what, like three or four more? I did the math. If I encountered one dirty butt per year, that's like twenty-five dirty butts I'd be elbows deep in before I'd finally get to escape the hell this one decision would bring upon us. And think of the others!

If we did it, then everybody would have to do it. I'm pretty sure Ben Franklin himself established the no butt wiping rule when he invented the first fire department, and who was I to question Ben Franklin and hundreds of years of tradition that preceded me? I wasn't doing it. I couldn't do it. This was not my dog, and it sure wasn't my fight. What are you doing, Boz? Nope. It's not happening.

While I waded through the reasons for why I should stand my ground, there was one nagging feeling weighing on me. What *was* that? Guilt? I shouldn't feel guilty. Even the lady's own husband wouldn't do it. I had no responsibility to her. But then again, Boz felt *some* responsibility, and I have a responsibility to him. The guilt I was feeling wasn't the guilt of breach of duty to her, but the guilt of letting a captain do a dirty grunt job while we sat on the porch.

I looked over at the man, still smoking quietly in his chair. *I'm no better than that idiot*, I thought. I looked at Ryan and could see his inner monologue had gotten the best of him too. In unison, we looked at each other and said, "You know we can't let the captain do that by himself." We laughed at the thought we had even considered not participating, before donning a pair of gloves and heading back inside. "Give us that towel, Cap. We got it." He shrugged his shoulders, handed over the towel and exited to the porch.

The poop had dried into a crust, which had encapsulated the smell. At first it wasn't so bad, but with each wipe, the shell flaked off and exposed the fresher, more rancid layers. I was becoming nauseated. In the bathroom, I rang out the dirty towel into the sink and went back for another pass, but as I wiped, I felt the contents of my stomach climbing up my esophagus. I was about to erupt like Mt. St. Helens. I ran outside and leaned over our "thinking" rail and heaved my lunch into the bushes.

As I collected myself, I overheard the husband apologizing to Boz. "I'm sorry. I just can't do it. I'll throw up."

Boz, beside himself at this juncture, pointed to me as I returned to the hazmat zone. "So will he," he said. "And it ain't even his wife."

We finished the job and climbed back aboard the engine. "I wanna' thank you guys," Boz said. "For a moment there, I thought y'all were going to hang me out to dry, and I actually *was* going to have to do it!"

The Pheasant

"What the hell is that?" he asked, pointing to the grill of my 1999 Dodge Stratus. I looked down and was surprised to see a bird hanging by the neck. His head had been pressed between the slats of my grill, and he had become a semi-permanent hood ornament. I had a vague recollection of a thud as I drove down the road but didn't see anything and figured it must have been something bouncing up off the pavement and thought nothing more of it.

Garrett grabbed the bird by the body and attempted to extricate it, but it was stuck. "It's a damn pheasant," he remarked. I didn't have time for this. I was late for class and decided I would take care of it later.

Hours went by, and I had forgotten about the bird, but Garrett hadn't, thankfully. "I took care of the pheasant for you," he told me with a cigarette dangling from his mouth. Thank God. I was not looking forward to touching the thing. I thanked him, started my car, and went on my way.

Three July days had gone by, and I noticed my car had adopted a new funk. An aroma that was unpleasant but bearable. I inspected the grill for signs of pheasant remnants, but there was nothing obvious. I reasoned it must have been blood or feathers or something that had gotten into the engine compartment and was now wafting in through the vents. I washed the car and rolled down the windows to air out.

Another day or two went by, and the smell became unbearable. It was downright rancid. I again rolled down the windows and turned the AC on full blast.

As the car cooled down, the smell faded, and I was completely dumbfounded. It shouldn't have gotten better when I turned the air on if it was coming in through the vents. Unsatisfied with the results thus far, I completed another interior inspection and, again, found nothing. I was stumped.

By day seven, I couldn't take it anymore. The North Carolina summer heat was causing the stench to permeate my clothes, and I gagged as I stepped into the firehouse.

"Whatsamatter witchu?" Garrett asked.

"My car reeks, man. I can't figure out what it is," I said exasperated.

Garrett couldn't stop laughing. I didn't know what was so funny. "Go… go look underneath yo' passenger seat," he said in a fit of coughing and wheezing laughter.

I looked again but saw nothing. He pushed me out of the way, reached way up into the underside of the seat, and pulled out a plastic bag coated with a liquified goo and feathers. He untied the bag, and the stench was unleashed. I gagged, and we both vomited. The lesson? Never leave your car unlocked at the fire station.

Fire with Fire

Messing with the rookie is a pass time. For the rookie, being the butt of the joke is a rite of passage. There are but two rules in the rookie hazing game. Never mess with a firefighter's gear, and never mess with their bedding. The second rule is somewhat flexible when it comes to rookies, so just to be safe, I purchased black sheets, pillowcases, and blankets. I had heard the stories of waking up to go on a call and showing up with the side of your face covered in flour or glitter after it was hidden in the victim's sheets. I was intent on not being an easy target. There is a third rule for rookies—accept the prank with grace, laugh with the guys, and clean up the mess when it's done. I would do all of that if they got me, but I didn't intend to make it easy.

For weeks, I had been anxiously waiting for the moment to come. I had taken steps to thwart these attempts on my pride. I ensured I was the last to bed and made my bed in the dark. If my bed was not made, they could not get me. I opened my locker slowly in case someone had decided to fill it with rubber snakes or a glitter bomb. I refused to poop at the station. There is no more vulnerable position in a fire station than the stall of a bathroom with your pants around your ankles, and I would not be caught with my pants down. I showered rapidly, and after most had gone to bed in case someone wanted to throw ice water over the top or cut off the hot water and steal my clothes.

For all of this caution, nobody seemed interested. Nobody had even made so much as an attempt to get me. I began to convince myself all the stories we heard in the academy were probably just to scare us, and this firehouse just didn't roll that way. I was a little disappointed.

As Ike and I walked through Walmart, we were delighted to find a pallet of silly string. "Let's buy a couple and silly string the Lieutenant," he suggested. I was down. We hatched a plan to unleash it on him after we got in the truck. It was a stupid stunt that barely qualified as a prank. However, this was unheard of. A rookie messing with the Lieutenant? It had to be a set up, and I saw it coming from a mile away. But, if this was as bad as it got, maybe I could finally relax.

We loaded the groceries and took our seats in the truck. Ike had given the keyword, and at that moment, I would silly-string him from the back, and Ike would do it from the driver's seat, or so he said. I knew he wasn't going to, and I would be hung out to dry as the dumb rookie who silly-stringed a Lieutenant. It was so obvious.

We put on our headsets, the Lieutenant strapped himself into the seat, and the moment arrived. Pineapple. The keyword was pineapple. I shoved my hand through the makeshift sallyport and unleashed a full can of slimy, squishy, air compressed, silicone-based silly-string upon the man who made the decisions that decided whether I lived or died. Peeking into the front seat to admire my work, I realized Ike had missed an opportunity. There the lieutenant sat, coated in two different colors of silly string.

I had not been hung out to dry after all. Ike was bummed at the missed opportunity when I told him of what I believed was going to happen. The lieutenant was not amused. "Really? A rookie playing pranks?" he scoffed. I laughed, but he was deadly serious. My laughter faded into a nervous chuckle, and then to awkward silence. For the remainder of the trip back, nobody said a word. I realized I had opened pandora's box.

A week later, I was hunting for my hard collared uniform shirt. I had been reassigned to the engine for the day, and the ladder was out of the station. I checked in all the usual places, but it was nowhere to be found. I felt my phone buzz in my pocket and opened it to find it was Lieutenant BJ.

Look up, read the message.

Doing laps around the station, I checked everywhere that it could have possibly been. I poked my head up into the ceiling tiles, checked the rafters of the truck bay, and on top of the engine. I still couldn't find it. At a loss, I messaged him back.

Higher, came the reply.

How much higher could it be? With only one place higher than I looked, I went outside behind the station, and from the top of a telephone pole, twenty feet up, hung my shirt from a burnt-out light. My phone buzzed again.

Ladder training when we get back.

He had gotten me, and like a scorned four-year old, *I* was telling. Ike and I went straight to the captain and told Boz of my predicament. "You know, we put that pole up back in the day when we used to play volleyball back there. We've been meaning to take that thing down for years," he pondered.

Was that a suggestion? I wasn't quite certain. "Can we cut it down?" I asked.

He stood up without saying a word, walked into his bunkroom, and closed the door behind him. From behind the door, I heard the words I needed to hear. "I see nothing." That was all the approval I needed.

Ike and I went back out, fired up the chainsaw, and began cutting through the creosote-soaked telephone pole. After burning through a few blades, it finally gave way and slammed into the ground, leaving only a stump where the pole had stood for almost two decades. I picked up my shirt and put it on, snapped a selfie, and sent it over to BJ. The reply was almost instant.

How'd you get it down? he wanted to know.

Thinking it better to let him stew, I said nothing.

Hours later, he returned to find the fallen pole lying on the ground. He was furious and wanted me written up, but now it was Boz's turn to teach. "What are you going to tell them when he explains why he cut it down?" BJ had no answer. "You can't write someone up for responding when you started it," Captain Boz explained. BJ stormed out of the office and didn't speak to me for three days, which didn't stop me from planning my next move in the war.

Not long before I had arrived, BJ had been promoted to lieutenant and assigned to the ladder. With his new role, came a shiny new helmet. We had finally had a fire, and he got to dirty it up. Before we began to take cancer seriously and were able to attribute so many cases to the contents of the smoke on our gear, firefighters used to wear a dirty helmet like a badge of honor that signaled to the world how much fire you had seen.

Someone suggested it was the rookie's job to clean the Lieutenant's helmet. I knew better, but I'd play along. I just saw an opportunity to mess with him again and blame it on someone else. Afterall, I was just the dumb rookie who didn't know any better. I took some Windex and spit polished that thing. The soot hadn't had time to bake in and permanently stain the surface yet, so getting it back to its bright cherry red was no task at all. As far as I was concerned, I had done him a service, but I had also violated rule number one, in the name of safety, of course.

Again, he was angry but could do nothing. The policy *was* to wash your gear after every fire, and I had not messed with his gear in such a way as to render it dangerous. In fact, I had done just the opposite. Boz was old school and, cancer be damned, told me that if I touched *his* helmet, he'd transfer me to the medic permanently. BJ decided since I liked cleaning so much, I could wash the windows. I considered this a small price to pay. The guys all laughed and grabbed towels to help me, amazed at the boldness of the rookie. I was fitting in, and I had managed to do what others had not. Nobody really messed with me anymore because I had developed a reputation for striking first and going bigger, but more importantly, I was building camaraderie with my new family. I slept a bit more soundly after that.

The Phantom Off Switch

Lieutenant Lackadaisical had pushed us to our limit one night. It was well into the wee hours of the morning, and his snoring barely eclipsed his blaring tv he had left on in the semi-communal bunkroom. We all lay awake staring at the flashing blue light on the ceiling and listened to the soothing sounds of battle scenes from whatever he was watching. Chris had had enough and set about doing God's work.

He gently opened the door and turned off the TV, and collectively, we all breathed a sigh of relief. Quietly, from a few bunks down, someone whispered, "Thank you!"

The next morning, Lieutenant Lackadaisical was annoyed and directed us not to turn off his TV. We played dumb. Nobody was going to rat out our savior. The next night, there was a repeat of the incident, and the lieutenant again issued a stern warning, but again, we had no idea what he was talking about. Certainly, he must have forgotten he had set his sleep timer, like a decent person would. On the third night, we repeated the process, but this time the lieutenant had booby trapped his door.

He had stacked several empty soda cans in front of the door so when the perpetrator entered, he would knock them over and be caught red-handed. Not to be outdone, Chris had somehow become wise to the alarm and devised a new technique. He opened the circuit breaker and shut off the power to the bunkroom, and then flipped it back on. The tv turned off, and the power was restored. LL was baffled.

He was convinced we had a universal remote, so on the following day, he put a piece of electrical tape over the sensor. That should do it. It didn't. Electrical tape has no effect on central wiring. Now anger surpassed annoyance, and the tattletale brought it up in the morning meeting, in front of Captain Boz. Boz has no patience for this nonsense and made a new rule, TV off by 10 PM in the bunkroom, almost like a decent person would do without being told. We won the battle, and he never learned how we beat him, until he reads this book, I suppose.

Of course, we didn't always go big. There are the dumb games we played like the cinnamon dragon, aptly named for the reaction of the unfortunate victim. You bet someone they can't eat a tablespoon of cinnamon. It's a safe bet because it is impossible. If they fall for it, it's usually about three seconds of misplaced confidence followed by widened eyes and sheer terror as the powdered spice sucks every drop of moisture in their mouth, and the dust invades their lungs and nasal cavities. The burn becomes intense and causes a violent dusty burst outward as they begin to cough while trying to rake it off their tongue. It usually results in a fit of coughing, tears, and snot running down their face as the spice infiltrates every cavity.

Like brothers, we all laugh at the expense of the victim. In a well thought out version of this prank, someone has preemptively turned off the water in the station so when they run to the sink to replenish the moisture in their mouth, nothing comes out, worsening the agony for the victim. Disclaimer: There are documented cases of death as a result of this prank. We had to cease this shenanigan once that little tidbit came out. One would think that as supposed experts in anatomy and physiology, asthma, breathing disorders, etc., we would be smarter than to subject our brethren to this. One would be wrong, but with age comes wisdom. Heed my advice. Don't do it.

There's also the spoon game where you bet the new guy you can beat him in a game of spoons, explaining the rules as follows: You each have a wooden spoon in your mouth while the other bends over and lets his opponent hit him in the back of the head. Then it's the other guys turn. The first guy to bow out, loses. The caveat is the victim doesn't know there is someone standing behind him with a large metal spoon, and when he bends over and thinks the other guy is hitting him with the spoon in his mouth, the guy behind him whacks him hard in the head with the metal spoon. A tough victim will last about three rounds before he can't take anymore, and then we all laugh at his goose egg.

Finally, there is the ladder pull up and lock. You tell the rookie it's a physical fitness challenge that simulates their ability to self-extricate off a roof in a pinch by doing a pull-up and locking off onto one of the rungs with the carabiner attached to a ladder belt. Eager to prove their physical fitness, they do so enthusiastically and are usually impressed with how easily they were able to accomplish the task.

The pull up is easy since they're fresh out of the academy and have done thousands of them. Locking the carabiner off on the rung while holding yourself up with the other hand is a bit tougher, but most can easily accomplish the goal. Then they let go, and we all cheer at their amazing show of physical prowess, except for the guy who runs up with the water hose to soak him down while he dangles there helplessly and the other guy with a bag of flour to turn him into the Pillsbury dough boy. Getting down is impossible once the weight of the body is pulling down on the carabiner lock, so he, in his dough covered glory, is left there to dangle for a few minutes, trying to figure it out until he is completely exhausted. Only then do we extend mercy and return with a ladder to finish the job.

These are the games we play. They may seem childish, better suited for high school or the playground, but they play an important role. It builds camaraderie and trust amongst family, and they *are* family. You spend a third of your life with these folks, and their family becomes your extended family. You do things together outside of work. Your kids become friends. You watch their kids grow up and adopt the title of uncle. You serve as the best man in their wedding, and then tell them you never liked her anyway when they divorce. You grieve together when one of your own suffers and provide support on the hard days.

These games help us dance the line between total burnout and being okay. They lighten the mood after a dark day. They help us deal with problem children, teach us lessons in conflict resolution, equalize the balance of power, and are an olive branch to the rookie as we induct them into the family. These games are not games at all. These are stress reducing, team building, family creating activities.

CHAPTER 9

IT'S GETTING PRETTY HAIRY

In the wake of September 11, Americans were gut punched by the images of jumpers who chose to leap to their deaths over leaving their fate to the flames. Twenty-four hours per day, we were inundated with video of airliners piloted by the embodiment of evil smashing into skyscrapers, which subsequently crashed to the ground, entombing their occupants.

Through all the dismay, anger, sadness, shock, and all the other emotions we experienced, we sat in awe of fire crews, police officers, and paramedics who worked around the clock in an effort to rescue whatever survivors remained and restore order to a city brought to its knees. The now famous image of a group of firefighters raising the American flag atop "the pile" became the symbol of American pride and spirit. At a time when we felt hopeless, this image gave us hope.

Firefighters have always sat at the top of the hero list and have captured the imaginations of children since Ben Franklin created the first fire department, but before this day, I don't believe the public had any idea what the job actually entailed. That is, until they witnessed these men and women running into a building everyone else was fighting to escape. That line is as cliché as they come, but it remains true.

The public showed up in force to express their support of the ongoing rescue effort. They lined the streets with food and water to replenish depleted bodies and bathing stations to clear the dust and grime from exhausted rescuers. They cheered on the rescue effort as firefighters and rescue workers came and went. They joined the lines and passed buckets of debris down from person to person off the pile. They sacrificed their time and money to help their fellow man in whatever way they could. They appreciated the job, and they appreciated each other. America was good.

"Never Forget" became the mantra of the nation, but guess what? They forgot. They not only forgot, but they created a new enemy out of these people. After September 11th, there was some leftover "hero" capital that lasted for around a decade, but soon enough, that was spent. In my early career, I remember being thanked often. I remember people buying my meals when I went out to a restaurant and stopping to talk when we went to the grocery store. I didn't need or want any of this, but it *was* kind of nice to at least feel appreciated. I'm not sure when the change occurred or if I just became more acutely aware of it as I got older, but sometime after the death of my son, I just got really sick of people. It felt like the joy in the job was gone overnight. People became mean.

Assault on Fire and EMS workers has been on the rise for a decade or more. According to *EMS World Magazine*, "52% of EMS workers report having been injured as the result of an assault while on the job. More than 20% report it as a primary concern but, for some reason, this is still not considered a priority by EMS executives, researchers, educators or practioners." To make matters worse, it is believed these assaults are underreported, and in reality, I believe they are downplayed as "just part of the job."

Anecdotally, we began to hear stories of gangs calling in false calls and ambushing firefighters with gunfire as they arrived on scene, and EMS crews being shot while caring for their patients. This was not an entirely new phenomenon. I have been assaulted and insulted throughout my career, but the intensity of these events seems to have escalated in recent years.

When folks would ask me, "Aren't you scared of going into a fire?" I always responded, "Not as scared as I am of people. Fire is mostly predictable. It burns up and out until it burns down. With people, you never know what they will do."

I used to be mostly unphased by the unknowns. I had a good demeanor and felt I could teach a mouse to love a starving rattlesnake. The kicker is sometimes you've got to be the mouse and sometimes the snake. I developed an acute street awareness and learned what worked in urban communities. I knew what it took to gain their respect, and I knew how to get the job done in hostile situations. In isolation, these events are mostly manageable—not always, but mostly.

What seems to have changed is the collective of public thinking and the willingness to believe almost anything that suits the narrative while ignoring the facts entirely. This line of thinking is spurred on by politicians and news media with self-interests that strongly align with ongoing public chaos. Afterall, it makes for great news, and a good politician will never let a crisis go to waste. They sit atop their thrones, looking down at all of us, and grandstand about their understanding of your plight and their grand plans to fix it, while not giving it two seconds of thought beyond the photo op.

They chastise police and public safety for doing the job they are paid to do with no understanding of the job themselves. This spurs the mob to action. Rather than stepping in to do the right thing, they record every event on their iPhones and hurl insults at police and medics without knowing a single fact about the case. It doesn't matter the reason for the arrest or who the person has hurt, if a police officer is involved, he or she is the bad guy. Not wanting to be the next face on the news or often under orders from their political superiors, police have backed off and now only intervene reluctantly, often leaving the offenders uncharged, particularly in the wake of COVID where prosecutors are unwilling to hold the offenders in jail under the guise of keeping jail populations low.

This does not just affect cops but has bled over into all aspects of public safety. As the prevalence of the Black Lives Matter movement gained steam, in Indianapolis we had a brief stint of vandalism and rioting that lead our leadership to advise against using certain routes and avoid going downtown. We received notifications to our phones about spontaneous demonstrations and protests popping up that would block ambulance routes and were advised to wear ballistic vests on all calls, lest the "peaceful" protest turn violent. There was a very real fear of becoming surrounded by an angry mob. This wasn't what I signed up for and made it really difficult to keep going to work. For this reason, I think it's important the stories of these incidences be told.

Chaos in the Projects

In 1940, America had begun to mobilize for a war. Portsmouth Naval Shipyard sits nestled on the banks of the Elizabeth River, which drains into the Atlantic Ocean, and across the river, is Norfolk, home of the world's largest naval base. As the country ramped up the war effort, Portsmouth was flooded with shipbuilders and military personnel. The growing numbers of men and their families needed places to live, so the US Housing Association rapidly erected cement block apartments.

These structures were designed to last for five to ten years or for the duration of the war, whichever came first. Durable construction would be a waste of manpower and material we didn't have to waste in a time when the country was being rationed. At the conclusion of the war, the military began to demobilize and sent the workers and service members home, leaving these temporary structures vacant. The city saw an opportunity to house its low-income residents, which in 1945, was a fancy way of saying "Black folks."

Through decades of segregationist policy and the vicious cycle of poverty and violence, these people saw little upward mobility, and today, these five-to-ten-year structures now stand as the projects of Portsmouth. In 2008, these semi-temporary structures had changed little and lacked modern amenities such as air conditioning and electricity, but for those with low income, beggars can't be choosers, and these structures were filled with nearly 100 percent minorities who were destined to repeat the cycle of the projects.

Shootings and stabbings were the norm in these neighborhoods. From the time I began considering Portsmouth as an employer, I had listened to old-timers lament about how they used to carry mag lights back in the day to "break heads" if necessary and would only enter under escort of police, but those days were now gone.

One night, the bell summoned us to the report of a breathing difficulty in one of the projects, medic only. The notes said nothing about concern for scene safety or the crowd that had gathered at this location, and so my partner and I gave it no thought until we arrived. In front of us stood dozens of people, and behind us, the exit was accessible only by backing out, which was no longer an option. We would never make it before being surrounded. We sat for a moment and stared ahead, trying to figure out what to do. The crowd became impatient with our hesitation and started walking toward us. Our decision had been made for us.

I stepped out, grabbed my bags and radio, and moved into the crowd, but their rigid postures and balled up fists did not change. My partner began to assess the patient, who was clearly having an anxiety attack, as I stood guard, keeping tabs on any threats in the crowd. Almost instantly, we were surrounded, and I could no longer focus my attention in any one direction. Things were starting to get hairy.

The crowd became more and more hostile, yelling and pushing, and suddenly, I was struck in the back, knocking me off balance. The biggest guy in the crowd shoved me and forcefully explained I had better help his little cousin, or he would kill me. The anger within began to boil, and I had had enough. I have always been non-confrontational, but on this night, something snapped inside of me. I think I was running purely on survival instinct.

I pulled my radio out and called for police assistance, knowing if this went much further, we were going to be hurt long before they arrived, and there was no escape. This situation required action. My partner, still focused on the patient, had not recognized the growing threat yet, or at least had not let on she had. It was up to me.

Shoving the bully with my empty hand and my radio in the other, I made a bold threat. "I am going to help her, but you had better back the fuck up before I shove this radio so far up your ass that you're going to taste it." The second it left my mouth, the crowd moved in, and I knew that I was about to die, but instead, something interesting happened.

"Oh, we good bro. We good," reconsidered the bully. The adage about standing up to the bully proved true. I learned something there. Reason was not going to work amidst that chaos, but this was a group that spoke the language of aggression and violence, and on this night, I had learned I was fluent. I had spoken in terms they understood, and in doing so, had demonstrated I was not afraid of them (even though I was terrified), and I was working in the interest of their friend to the point I was willing to fight the biggest guy in the crowd to help her. My gamble worked.

From that point on, the bully became an ally. He adopted a new role, that of crowd control. As I tapped my partner on the shoulder and indicated we needed to go, he pushed them back, consoled them, and redirected their energies. Not all were swayed though. One guy called him out. "Man, fuck that. They ain't doing shit!" The bully had a new target. He stepped up to him, face to face, and said nothing. He simply looked him in the eye, arms at his side and jaw rigid, and there they stood, nose to nose, chest to chest. The detractor got the hint and stomped off.

The bully resumed his work. "Step back, y'all. They got this. She gonna be fine. Let 'em do they job." He was obviously someone they respected. We collected the patient, and the crowd split in front of us, no longer hostile, just worried. I stepped out of the truck and reassured them all would be fine, and we vacated the scene before there was another shift in attitude.

You Don't Know Who I Am

You never know who you're going to get when you arrive. It doesn't matter. The job is the same whether it's the President of the United States or this patient, a violent gang leader who is well-known to local law enforcement. Of course we didn't know that when we got the call for a head injury.

We arrived to find he had fallen and struck his head on the concrete. I squatted in front of him and began asking questions, but he was reluctant to answer, and what little he did say made no sense. He was showing signs of a concussion and was very confused. We explained he needed to see a doctor, but he didn't want to be transported. His pride did not permit it.

This was problematic for us. His altered mental state required us to transport him by law, so we disputed back and forth about the matter, trying to reason and explain our position. Eventually, he decided he was done talking and pulled his fist back to punch me. From my squatted position, I had two options, forward or backward, but I didn't have time to make decisions.

My decision was made when I chose to follow my training and stayed squatting rather than taking a knee. I could back up, but it was already too late, and I couldn't get away even if I wanted to. Doing so would allow him to get extension to apply the full force of the strike. Instead, I lunged forward and tackled him. Without hesitation, my crew followed suit and dogpiled on top of me, one holding his legs, another an arm, and someone else on the other arm. Boz, the only one with the wisdom to stay out of the fray, hit the 10-1 button, an orange button on the top of the radio that opens the mic and signals to the dispatcher we are in trouble, that is, when it works.

Dispatch tended to be complacent with the protocol, and this occasion was no different. They repeated their requests for us to clear the open mic over and over again. "Engine Ten, contact dispatch code one. Engine Ten, contact dispatch code one." There is a key phrase we are supposed to reply to clear the code, and if we don't say it precisely, they are supposed to send the cavalry, but they didn't. "Engine Ten, contact dispatch code one." Boz said nothing. "Engine Ten, contact dispatch code one." Finally, it was clear she was not going to follow the procedure and Boz got angry.

"We have a violent patient and need PD now. Send PD!" he demanded. A plainclothes female officer heard our call and soon arrived, but as Captain Bostic noticed her, there was nothing that indicated she was a cop. "Who are you?" he asked.

She explained she was a cop and came to assist because she recognized the address. She had no gun, no visible badge, and no pepper spray or handcuffs. Boz smirked. "Where is your gun and handcuffs?" he asked in his slow southern drawl. Reluctantly, she informed him she didn't have them with her. "Well, I appreciate you coming but that doesn't do me a whole hell of a lotta' good."

Another cop arrived, and the two of them took our patient into custody. We cleared the dogpile and transported a very angry man to the hospital with vowed threats to "end our lives," but I had talked to him. At that moment, he couldn't even remember his own name, so even though I now knew his criminal reputation, I wasn't worried about him remembering mine.

Out of Bed and Into the Fire

Bang, Bang, Bang! I awakened to the sound of someone beating on my door, at least I thought. The red light above my bed wasn't on, and I didn't hear the dispatcher talking over the speaker.

Shit, I thought to myself. I must have missed a call, or had I? If I had, it had been a while or the light would still be on, and I would still be hearing the dispatcher talking. Maybe I had dreamed it. It *had* been a busy day, and I *was* exhausted. It was certainly possible I had slept through one. I lay awake and listened for a moment, but I didn't hear anyone yelling for me in the hall.

Bang, Bang, Bang! There it was again. This time it was undeniable, but it didn't sound close. I got up and pulled on my pants and boots and opened the door. There was nobody there. Maybe my partner had given up trying to wake me and had gone back downstairs to tell the dispatcher his partner was missing and she should send another crew. That would mean my head on a stick. I had better hurry. *Bang, Bang, Bang!* What on Earth was going on?

I ran down the three flights of stairs, skipping steps along the way. In the stairwell, I met the Battalion Chief. "There's a gunshot wound on the front apron! I'll have dispatch tone it out," he yelled. So I didn't miss a call. The banging I had heard was a frantic bystander banging on the bay door three floors below my bed. I stepped outside, and the bay door was already opened with a large crowd gathered. Dozens of people frantically screamed at me to, "Put some pep in your step, mother fucker!" and, "Hurry up! He's dying!"

Rule number one of EMS is scene safety. We don't go where the scene isn't safe, and I knew nothing about this scene except that everyone was yelling at me. Three minutes prior, I was sound asleep in my bed. Now I was standing in front of dozens of angry people who placed the blame for their friend's condition squarely at my feet because I did not magically appear ready for life saving when they beat on my garage door in the middle of the night. I didn't know what lay outside except a hostile crowd and a man who was apparently shot.

On a normal call, I wouldn't have entered this scene, but I wasn't really given that choice. The scene was beneath my feet, and no matter where I went, that wouldn't change, so I grabbed a pair of gloves and went out to assess the situation. I was surprised to find I was the only one. Nobody but me and the battalion chief had heard the rapping on the door. I was alone with nothing in my hands but a pair of trauma shears on my belt. "Where is the guy that is shot?" I asked a man who had told me to "Hurry the fuck up."

"He's in the back of the truck."

I peeked around the back of the truck to find a man doing chest compressions on the victim. "What happened? Does anybody here know him?" I asked.

"Of course, I know him!" he screamed, turning over CPR responsibility to me.

I glanced over the patient, feeling for a pulse and found nothing. There was no rise or fall of the chest. He was not breathing. It was dark outside, and I couldn't see a thing.

"Where is he shot?" I asked.

"I don't know! I'm not a fucking doctor, man. That's your job!" the man screamed at me.

I reached into my pocket and pulled out my cell phone, turning on the flashlight. Shining it over the victim's body, I found a small bullet hole in the side of his neck and a large gaping wound on the opposite side of his head. I recognized there was little chance of surviving this wound, but I was not inclined to inform these people of that right now. I shined the light into the patient's eyes. His pupils were fixed and dilated, confirmation brain activity had ceased. This patient was dead, but I was still alone and didn't intend to face the ramifications of that by myself.

I began chest compressions. As I pumped, vomit spilled from the patient's mouth and blood and brain matter spurted from the hole in his head. This was an obviously futile effort. It was doing nothing to revive this man, but for now, I felt it was keeping the crowd as calm as could be expected. I began to wonder where the hell everyone was. It felt like it had been forever since I encountered the chief in the stairwell. Somebody should have joined me by then.

I looked around the scene and tried to find someone to tell me anything. I eyed the crowd suspiciously. For all I knew, the shooter was here right now, watching me work, perhaps even training the gun on me. Would he come back to finish the job? Would I be on his hit list now that I had attempted to save his victim?

"What happened? Who shot him?" I asked anybody who would listen.

"I don't know! We were just sitting at a stoplight, and somebody just came up and shot him. We drove off, and we didn't realize that he was hit until after we got away."

I probed further as I continued CPR. "Where did this happen?" He gave me a location. Finally, one of my guys arrived.

"What do you need?" he asked.

"Where the hell is my partner?" I demanded. He didn't know. "Stay here and do CPR. I'll be right back."

I headed back into the building to get my equipment, and at the bay entrance, found the entire crew and my partner standing there looking out into the crowd. "This guy is dead. We're working him as a formality until we can get out of here. I need the stretcher, and we're leaving," I relayed. The battalion chief was on board with my decision and people started to move, but finally a cop arrived.

I walked up to him and explained the victim was dead and there was nothing I could do. With a man with a gun finally on scene, I was finally comfortable with ending the charade and making the death pronouncement. I recorded time of death, told the crowd there was nothing more I could do in one of the least empathetic notifications possible, and retreated to the safety of the fire station, closing the bay doors behind me. Our fire station apron, thirty feet below my bed, was now the crime scene for a murder investigation.

I Got Something for Yo' Ass

"Sick person" calls are the single most common call of any EMS agency, and 95 percent of the time, they are routine, easy in and out, and back to the station. On this July evening, I was sent to a "sick person," an elderly male who was just not feeling well, and according to his wife, had not been eating. He was pleasant, and there was no cause for concern, so we went about the mundane task of putting him on the stretcher and moving to the ambulance.

I was standing in the truck and waiting for the guys to finish delivering him to my care when a car in the distance caught my attention. I waited for him to move over, but he didn't seem to be slowing, or moving for that matter. He was in our lane and seemed to be accelerating. "Watch out!" I yelled to my crew, but they had nowhere to go.

The car slammed on its brakes and came to a sliding stop no less than three feet from the butt of the guy holding the end of the stretcher. The driver jumped out, demanding to know what was wrong with his dad, and for a moment, we were relieved this was just a concerned family member and not some crazy person, but the feeling was short lived.

We attempted to calm him down, but he was angry for no discernible reason and not one to listen to reason. He tried to push his way into the back of the ambulance despite pleas from his father to stop and calm down. I pushed him back out and told him he was not allowed in the back of the truck, but he persisted and reaffirmed his intent to have his way. I had learned from the gang leader incident and hit the Code-1 button, but this time I told them I needed PD before they could even ask. Captain Boz, still inside gathering information from the patient's wife, heard my call and came out, confused. This was a sick person. How did this go south?

One of our guys on the ground grabbed the belligerent son by the belt and yanked him out while the other guys formed a defensive line in front of the doors of the ambulance. He was a short, skinny guy and the muscular blue wall in front of him had made him acutely aware of that fact. "Oh, it's like that, huh?" A rookie firefighter standing directly in front of him had the clear size advantage and smiled down on him. He realized the fight wasn't fair and decided to change things up. "That's fine. I've got something for yo' ass," he said as he ran toward the house.

"Leave, now!" Boz ordered.

The doors slammed shut, and we started down the road without even locking the stretcher into the latch. As we sped away, the stretcher slammed into the walls of the ambulance, and I did my best to fight the forces of the curves and push it into locking position. Finally, I was able to secure it and focused on the events unfolding outside. Behind me, the fire engine was running blocking maneuvers, swerving back and forth to prevent the assailant from passing and getting to the truck. Boz ordered the driver to keep him behind at any cost.

"What do I do if he gets by me?" the driver asked.

"Hit his ass. He can shoot through the back of that ambulance, but he can't shoot through this fire truck."

The chase continued down the road like this for a couple of miles, but the attacker made a move to take a side road and get in front of us. We continued, and Boz directed us to take an alternative route over the radio. Knowing where the side road came out, the engine sped past us to get in front of the assailant and pulled into the intersection to block traffic. They sat in the middle with their lights on, creating a roadblock with exiting interstate traffic and obstructed the assailant's path to the hospital until police, who had been across the city on a vehicle accident, arrived on scene. They ordered him out of the vehicle at gun point and searched the car, but found no weapon, so *they let him GO*! Twenty minutes later, he was at the hospital being held at bay by security. This became an interdepartmental scandal and caused a rift between the police chief and the fire chief.

This call was a prime example of how fast a seemingly benign scene can go south. I think there has been some recognition of the danger other humans pose to us in recent years, and departments have begun to take assault on EMS somewhat more seriously, but the solutions they provide are directed to calls where there is already police presence. That does me no good when an angry son shows up to a sick person call.

In the wake of the Michael Brown shooting, I remember serious discussion about changing our uniforms away from the hard collared, button-down shirts with the badge and name plate sewn on the front because we looked too much like cops. We would walk through the grocery store and kids would hide behind their parents or point us out and say "Look, a policeman!" We were indistinguishable to the public from the police despite our lack of guns and tasers.

There was a proposal to change our uniforms to red t-shirts with "FIRE" written on the back to make us more clearly identifiable. The administrative compromise was we were to take the hard collared shirts off after 5 PM and continue to wear blue. Apparently bad things only happen at night, and there was a lot of angst amongst the brass about the possibility of our professional image taking a hit if we were seen wearing a t-shirt. This irritated me at the time, but as public opinion has evolved, I don't think it would have mattered anyway.

We used to be a trusted part of the social fabric, but now, I think we are representative of a government which has done little to address citizen concerns, and they place that rage directly upon our shoulders. I don't think any greater respect is placed on Fire and EMS than Law Enforcement anymore. We get in just as many confrontations as they do.

Some departments are providing ballistic vests to wear onto scenes where shootings, assaults, or mentally unstable patients are waiting, but for as long as I've been in EMS, the rule has been we do not enter these scenes without the police declaring it safe first, so there is almost no point wearing the vest. These are not the calls where the bad stuff happens because the danger has already been mitigated. It's the sick person calls we must worry about, or the calls that happen thirty feet below your bedroom.

There have been laws passed in some states that allow first responders the right to carry a firearm while on duty. The problem is fire chiefs and public safety leaders are generally risk adverse to this idea. Instead of seriously considering the matter and offering self-defense and firearms handling classes, they shrug it off and say EMS possessing a firearm poses a greater danger to the public and to ourselves than the risks we regularly face. One of the common arguments I hear is, "What if someone takes it from you while you're taking care of the patient?"

To this, I reply, "Retention holsters exist. Lookout partners exist. Self-defense classes exist."

I have already cited several personal examples where having a gun would have been preferable to not having a gun. In my view, we are running scared, and it is time to take the matter seriously and equip our people with the skills and tools to defend themselves because these scenes turn in an instant. When you are about to be killed, nobody can save you except you. Presently, we don't have the tools to do so. However, the evidence is mounting that maybe we should.

In December of 2020, in Pine Bluff, Arkansas, paramedics were dispatched to the report of an injured knee. What they didn't know at the time was the injury was the result of an assault by the patient's boyfriend. While treating the patient, the boyfriend became angry, and the medics were assaulted. When one of the paramedics defended himself, the boyfriend pulled out a gun and opened fire, wounding both medics. One of the paramedics had a firearm and returned fire, killing the gunman. Both medics were seriously wounded, but survived, as well as the victim.

At this time, it is not clear whether this agency had a weapons policy or if the medic would have been in violation. If I was a betting man, I would say he was in violation of the policy. I have never heard of a department that allowed weapons to be carried while on duty. In response to the incident, a bill was intro-duced that would make it legal for first responders to carry a firearm in the course of their duties. However, it explicitly states the ability to do so would still be based on the agency's weapons policy, so in essence, the law did nothing. It's just another empty symbolic gesture from a politician. But hey, we're used to those by now, aren't we?

These are some of the headlines I have come across over the last several years. This is becoming an entirely too frequent occurrence. A simple Google of the words "Firefighter" or "Paramedic Shot" yields several pages of these results.

June 25, 2018. NBC Los Angeles.
Two Firefighters shot in Long Beach, California.
One Firefighter fatality.
Firefighters were responding to report of an explosion
at a senior living home.

December 24, 2012. BBC News.
US Firefighters shot dead at New York blaze.
Firefighters were responding to the report of a residential
structure fire in Webster, New York.

May 16, 2019. ABC News.
Firefighter shot to death responding to medical call was
father of 3 young kids.
Firefighters were responding to report of a seizure on a bus.

February 21, 2021. NBC KCRA.
Firefighter and Paramedic shot in drive-by while
responding to a call.
They were simply responding to a call.

If this was a TV show in the 90s, we would see a freeze frame, the "Skkkr-rrrrrttt" sound effect, and the main character stopping to talk to the camera directly. Several months after what I felt like was completion of this chapter, intensifying hostility toward EMS led me to buy a small .380 pistol I could keep in my pocket while at work. I had already been carrying pepper spray for months. Though not explicitly forbidden, it probably had me in murky waters with departmental policy. I figured the worst-case scenario was they would find out and I would be terminated, and the best case was it might one day save my life. I was already long past burnt out so termination didn't seem so bad.

My wife cautioned me against carrying the gun out of fear I would get attacked and have it used against me, or worse, given my declining mental health, get into an altercation where I would lose my head and use it unjustifiably. She viewed it as a greater risk. We went back and forth, and I saw validity in her concerns. I carry a firearm in every facet of my everyday life, but I've always been able to avoid conflict and had the ability to disengage if things escalated. The firearm is a last resort, as it always should be.

When you are treating a patient, disengagement is not always possible, and tempers can flare. Once, while treating a belligerent drunk patient who was in police custody for attempted murder, he spat in my face. I saw red. My blood boiled. Reason went out the window, and my muscles reacted viscerally. He was handcuffed to the stretcher and completely defenseless. I raised my Toughbook computer over my head and felt it accelerate toward his skull. It was nothing but divine intervention and air resistance that stopped that Toughbook computer from sinking into his forehead, sparing us both from the repercussions of such an action. It is in this scenario where I saw validity in my wife's concerns, but nevertheless, I stopped. I felt I had proven to myself in that situation I had the ability to exercise restraint.

As the Bible says, "Who can find a virtuous woman? For her price is far above rubies, The heart of her husband safely trusts in her and he will have no need of spoil." Basically, that means if a husband trusts in the wisdom and counsel of his wife, she will save him from making the dumb decisions us men so often make, which leads to hardship and financial ruin. God knows women have the risk-o-meter that was apparently not available in version 1.0. Heeding her wisdom, despite feeling I was capable of remaining rational, I decided to take some time and think the decision to carry the pistol through a bit further. I voiced to her, "Well that really leaves me in a bind. I'm damned if I do, and damned if I don't."

"I know," she replied. "You just need to focus on getting out of that job."

Two days after buying the pistol, this chapter got a bit more personal, which has led to the post-script addendum I have now included. A friend, name withheld for privacy's sake, responded to a call for wires down. A tree had fallen on some powerlines. After mitigating the hazard, while packing up to leave the incident, the neighbor arrived home. There was previous animosity between the two neighbors and an argument ensued before deteriorating into a fight.

My friend called for police and began to evacuate his guys from the scene, content to let the men fight it out. As the saying goes, "Not my monkey, not my circus," but before he could leave, one of the men was knocked down, and the agressor began to wail on the other man's wife. Unwilling to leave a man to assault a woman, my friend intervened, locked the assailant into a rear naked choke, and dragged him backwards. The woman's husband rose, drew a firearm, and fired two shots into them. One 9-millimeter round struck my friend in the elbow, damaging his ulnar nerve and deadened his arm. The second struck the neighbor. They both were treated at the hospital, and both survived.

Upon learning of this, I felt I really should carry the gun, but the pause I had agreed to had made something abundantly clear to me. My job would require me to go into schools, federal buildings, and other places where firearms are prohibited. Without the protection of the law, I could not do so and remain law abiding, so while I was willing to risk my job, I was not willing to risk my freedom or my status as a law-abiding citizen, so I set the gun aside and never made it a part of my every day carry at work.

In the coming days, the fire chief did not visit his man in the hospital. He did call three days later after outrage in the department became so great he felt he needed to do something to save face. When perceptions did not improve, he issued a departmental email to explain the city required his leadership during those three days, and he had spent them in the emergency operations command center. At the end of the email, in bold lettering, he scribed the department's core values. A perfect ending to a perfect cop out. The mark of a true academic leader. Public safety is full of this type of leader. These are people who have taken all the classes and gotten all the degrees and extra letters behind their name that would vault them to the top, but rarely have they any experience in what it means to actually lead people. For the most part, they are politicians.

By now, it should be clear I am frustrated with public safety leadership. I've provided a lot of a criticism, but I have always said to present a problem without a solution is nothing more than whining. This one is easy to solve. Create laws that protect first responder rights to protect themselves and make departments liable for their policies that restrict those rights. At present, they have no incentive to create policies allowing providers to defend themselves and every incentive not to. That needs to change and can be accomplished by making the risks and liability of creating such a policy greater than the risk of being sued in the absence of one.

It has worked for firefighters. Firefighters have some of the highest cancer risk of any profession due to the carcinogens contained within smoke. It also causes heart and lung disease. As a result, the International Association of Firefighters (IAFF) lobbied for legislation that makes departments responsible for disability payments under an "assumption act," which assumes these illnesses were contracted while on the job. Knowing they were on the hook, departments began to mandate Self Contained Breathing Apparatus (SCBA) usage, purchased extra sets of turnout gear and gear washers, and required gear to be washed after every fire. They had vent systems installed that sucked truck exhaust from the buildings, created wellness programs and physical fitness standards, established "No Tobacco" policies, required all new hires to sign a contract agreeing not to use tobacco substances, added slow wake up alert systems to reduce the stress on the heart from suddenly waking up to an alert bell, and so on and so forth. When you hurt their budgets, change happens. If legislators would mandate departments be responsible for the death or serious injury of their employees, we could equalize the risk departments face from being sued by the public with the risk they face of being sued by their own employees.

We also need to demand more from our police officers to put an end to the epidemic of assault on EMS. In most states, assaulting an EMS worker is a felony charge, but it seems like it is rarely enforced. In my scenario described earlier, where the patient spit in my face, my restraint was not met with gratitude. He saw it as a sign of weakness and began to taunt me. "Ohhh, you hit me! I'm gonna tell the cop that you hit me, and you're going to jail."

When we arrived at the hospital, I relayed this to the police officer and informed him I wished to press charges. The officer informed me the patient's significant other had told them he was HIV+, so there was a possibility my patient might be too. There is an extremely low risk of transmission of HIV from saliva and no risk unless it enters the mucosal membranes, but I had to be tested, which took me off the street for several hours. Guess what never happened? There was never a charge filed for assault on an EMS worker. That is two times assaulted, two times where I expected justice, and two times where none was delivered.

Through all these incidents, perhaps the most damaging thing I have encountered is a severe distrust of people. I worry as I pull up to a stop light that the person I am pulling up next to may be pursuing a gang initiation challenge to kill a paramedic and see the moment as the perfect opportunity to do the job and get away. I fear a crazy person will walk up to my wife and shoot her in the head for no reason as she exits her car with my kids. I always know my nearest exit point. I calculate shot distances at my church and consider where people would be running in the event of a mass shooter so I can avoid hitting them. I sit where I can see the entire auditorium.

My kids are entirely too aware of the evils of the world, and I require them to carry ballistic inserts in their backpacks so that in the event, God forbid, they face a school shooter, they have at least some means of protection. They have been taught the dos and don'ts of firearm safety, and my oldest has been taught to shoot. They are also skilled in Tae Kwon Do and have been given strict instructions to trust their gut if something doesn't feel right. These are knowledge, skills, and abilities we should all possess, but carrying this heightened sense of alertness around, this unnatural suspicion of people at all times, is exhausting.

Sometimes, I just wish I could bury my head to the things I've seen and go back to being that privileged, middle-class boy whose biggest fear was being rejected when asking a girl to the prom. The world doesn't stop being evil when you pretend the evil doesn't exist, but it sure was more pleasant when I was ignorant to it. Sadly, even after I leave the street, I am not certain I can ever "unknow" what I know. "On edge" may be my default mode for the rest of my life.

CHAPTER 10

PUT A MUZZLE ON IT

When you picture a firefighter, what do you see? My guess is it's the TV firefighter with a sharp jaw line, massive biceps, and a go with the flow, "Sure thing, Chief! Whatever you say!" attitude. I see someone with a lot to say, but nobody to listen.

For fire administrations, it's all about the perfect image. The rot beneath doesn't matter as long as the chief doesn't have to stand in front of any cameras and answer questions. There is no place in public safety for an individual opinion. Toe the line, keep your mouth shut, and be happy you're getting a paycheck, and if you don't like it, I can find a dozen more that are willing to take your place.

There is only one problem with that. We're the ones immersed in the problem. Not just *the* problem but *all* of the problems. We see it all. We see every side of every argument through all walks of life. We meet rich, poor, democrat, republican, good, bad, legal and illegal, foreign and natural born, sick and well, crackhead and church pastor, and crackhead *church* pastor. You name it, we have interacted with it. We are in your homes, underneath the overpass in the tent city, on the front lines of dealing with the opioid crisis, and the atrocity our veterans call their healthcare system.

We deal with mental illness, alcohol abuse, and the impact on the families. We see the good in humanity and the worst acts humans perpetuate on each other. I would venture to say we have the most well-rounded perspective on the problems America faces of any group of people in the country, and yet we dare not speak on it out of fear of retribution from our employers. Cancel culture is alive and well in public safety, and keeping the chief off of the news is our mission.

"You are held to a higher standard. If you mess up, you will find yourself in a newspaper with the headline 'Firefighter charged' or 'Paramedic terminated after…' next to your picture and a half page article." These are the lessons we are taught in the fire academy. That makes sense. Firefighters, paramedics, and police are role models. Little kids look up to us, so I can certainly understand the necessity of protecting that image when it comes to criminality.

What I cannot understand is the necessity of censoring our speech. As a matter of fact, I don't understand this for any job, let alone for people that should be consulted for solving every problem known to man, but in the modern political climate, listing my employer on my social media or posting a picture of myself in uniform is a serious risk. I am not disciplined enough to not call BS out when I see it, and if I do, you can bet someone will send a screenshot to my employer. That's fine. As I have gotten older, I have learned there is wisdom in the adage it is better to remain silent and be thought a fool, than to open your mouth and remove all doubt. But if someone asks, you can bet I will tell you what I think.

I learned this lesson the hard way. I believe I was somewhere around seven years into my career when I was plucked off the training ground by the deputy chief and shuttled downtown to his office. My heart raced as I thought about what I might have been in trouble for, but when he showed me a cartoon video and asked if I made it, I cannot explain the level of confusion that washed over me. This was a video I vaguely remembered making several years earlier about the assumptions people have about the fire and EMS profession and the stupid things they say.

At the time, one of the complaints administration said they received related to the usage of the fire truck to go to the grocery store, as well as parking in the fire lane. I remember some discussion about prohibition of using trucks to go to the grocery store. Fortunately, the captains were so obstinate, administration backed down to save themselves the riot. That is how ridiculous and out of touch some of these chiefs are. They were so worried about a citizen complaint, they completely overlooked the fact people have to eat over the course of twenty-four hours.

Around this time, there was a video circulating of an old man harassing a group of firefighters loading groceries into the fire truck because he was not happy they chose to shop at a cheaper grocery store further from their station rather than shop at the closer one where they would pay double. He was extremely worried about his tax dollars paying for the extra fuel and truck maintenance. In the video, firefighters exhibited exceptional professionalism while they endured the ridiculous rant.

My video was a parody of this event in which the firefighters actually said what they were thinking. It provided logical reasoning behind things like this and portrayed the citizen as a low life who didn't pay taxes. Let's face it, most people who worry about things like this have so much time on their hands from being unemployed and friendless, they stew on trivial matters and make issues out of nothing. Admittedly, my video was vulgar. As the chief put it, "This was the most disgusting, vulgar thing that I have ever seen in all my years." I highly doubt that Chief, but I digress.

The punishment was overblown but could have been worse. They wanted to see my response to the big reveal. They wanted to see if I would lie about it. I didn't, so three days later I was called back to the office and sat in front of the big man. I have to say I think he was reasonable. I later learned the city attorney had demanded I be terminated, so to save my job, he doled out a ten-day, unpaid suspension. I had recently been accepted onto the SWAT team as a SWAT Medic, and when they learned of the suspension, I lost my spot, which was probably what I was most upset about.

They didn't even know the circumstances surrounding the disciplinary action as it was a personnel matter, but they cut ties anyway. The fire service is basically high school. When my peers learned of my suspension, the rumors swirled. My reputation took a nosedive as they speculated. When I finally told them, their response was, "That's it?" Yep, that's it.

Boz was angry when he learned of the disciplinary action. He lobbied for the financial ramifications of the suspension to be delayed by two weeks to allow me time to get my affairs in order and became something of an attorney on my behalf. They honored this request, and he encouraged me to appeal the decision, citing errors they had made in the process. My municipality had a progressive disciplinary policy, starting with a verbal warning, written warning, one-day suspension, three-day suspension, five-day suspension, and ultimately ten-day suspension, and then termination. He noted they skipped all of them and progressed straight through to the most serious action, while I had an otherwise stellar record.

By comparison, shortly after my ordeal, a captain was found to have sent an unsolicited picture of his genitals to a female employee on his city issued cell phone and only received a three-day suspension. I had never so much as received a verbal reprimand prior to this incident and this captain got away virtually scot-free in a city with a zero-tolerance sexual harassment policy. Boz also questioned how they even discovered this video and why a video produced on my personal time was subject to disciplinary action at work.

How did they discover this, anyway? Upon further investigation, we learned a year earlier, a complaint had been made by a citizen about a post I had made on Facebook that had offended this person. Apparently they investigated me for a year and found nothing actionable until they discovered my YouTube channel. There would have been absolutely nothing they could do about this video except I had a profile picture of me in my Class A uniform, which was the justification they used for the disciplinary action. This was weak at best because you could not determine who my employer was based on the photo, but it was good enough for them.

Boz encouraged me to appeal the decision, but if I am being completely honest, I was embarrassed by the ordeal. I had made far more money by working my part time job during my time off, and I just wanted to get back to normal, so I elected to just let it go. It stuck with me for the duration of my time there though and left a sour taste in my mouth for my leadership. I didn't feel like they had my back.

Shortly after my suspension, the annual awards ceremony took place, and my crew and I cleaned up. A chief known for holding grudges had called my name so many times by the end of the night, that on the final award, a lifesaving award, he gritted his teeth and mumbled my name under his breath. I would be lying if I said I didn't take a little bit of pride in the obligatory handshake as he handed me the award. This was the beginning of the end of my time in this department. I began to see things for what they were, and once you become even a little bit jaded, it is hard to get the joy back you once had.

After this incident, I deleted the video. I deleted my employer and all photos on my social media that could possibly link me to the department. I changed my hometown so if someone somehow knew I was a firefighter/paramedic, they could not draw conclusions about where I worked. I stopped providing opinions from the perspective of a healthcare worker because as things became more politically charged, I realized they could potentially search my name, find out I was a medic, and use that information to determine where I worked. I lost faith in even those I considered to be friends and decided online debate wasn't worth my job. This is how one idiot can singlehandedly shut down useful debate and remove informed opinion from the discussion. Is it worth it? Sometimes I wonder.

CHAPTER 11
THE EPIDEMIC OF
SELFISH AND DUMB

I entered EMS as an idealist. In my world, adults behaved in a certain way, thought in a certain way, were responsible for their own actions, and made sacrifices to care for their children and themselves. It took me about seven minutes into my first shift to learn how wrong I was.

I grew up in lower middle-class white suburbia. My parents worked five or six jobs between them to keep us in that neighborhood. My dad left before the sun rose, stopped in at home to grab dinner before leaving again to work at whatever extra job he was working that night, and then returned around midnight and got up and did it all over again the next day. Mom was a medical transcriptionist. She worked from home, but in reality, she lived at work.

She would wake up at three or four in the morning and spend the day sitting at the computer transcribing whatever notes the physicians had on their patients for eight to twelve cents per line typed. The more she worked, the more she made, but hours in the day are finite, and she maximized every waking minute, often living on two or three hours of sleep. It was tedious, boring work that left her trying to decipher medical terms mumbled by doctors with foreign accents, but it provided the flexibility for her to be home when us kids got off the bus or were home for the summers.

They did this six days per week. The seventh was for church and rest, which, for my dad, meant dozing off in front of a NASCAR race or football game. We were blue collared common people. There wasn't a lot of money to go around, but we wanted for nothing and occasionally found the money to go on a family vacation or out to eat.

I abstained from pursuing a career in Virginia Beach because I viewed it as "rich people." I was offered multiple jobs from several agencies, two in one day, three or four within a week of each other, but I chose Portsmouth because it had a reputation for being lower income. I wasn't rich. I wanted to serve people that were like me—hard working, salt of the Earth, struggling to get by folks. I wanted to work for a community I could relate to. You can imagine the culture shock when the demographic I ended up serving was urban, 53.3 percent Black, 3.3 percent Hispanic, 2.6 percent biracial, 1.1 percent Asian, and 1.5 percent "other." Only 41.6 percent looked like me.

Furthermore, the crime rate in Portsmouth is 222 percent higher than the average for Virginia and 132 percent higher than national average. At present, almost a fifth of Portsmouth students will not graduate, but in 2010, Portsmouth had the worst graduation rate in the state with only 63.4 percent of its seniors graduating on time. If your experiences color your worldview, mine was decisively middle class and white. I had never experienced racism or had to worry about gangs. There weren't fights in my schools, not real fights anyway, and I had never worried about being shot for my shoes. I didn't have to worry about food insecurity or whether I was going to have to choose to pay my electric bill or get my medications.

I had no idea the problems that minority communities faced, but with such a high call volume, I began to pick up on the pulse of the community. I learned how to talk to them, gain their trust, what their problems were, and how to best address them. It wasn't easy though. I was still a middle-class white boy working in a poor minority community, and many viewed me as the reason for every problem. Many minority kids are taught to mistrust authority from a young age, perhaps deservedly so, and in me, they saw a badge and a blue uniform that came from somewhere else (very few of us lived in the city) and would leave to go back to where I came from after I got my paycheck. These are the stories of the calls that are so outlandish, so stupid, so ridiculous, that the average person often doesn't believe me when I tell them.

Take His Bed With You

I was working my part-time job at a private ambulance service and was on my twenty-sixth consecutive hour working with ten more to go, but this job was my playground. I didn't care about this job at all. In fact, I was embarrassed to tell people I worked there. I would never work at a place like this if there wasn't so little expected of me.

I wore my uniform *if* I wanted to. Nobody seemed to care if I did or didn't. I worked with my buddy, got the pick of shifts, and was given only three runs at the start of the day. What I did with the rest of my day was up to me. We usually spent it sitting at the mall or cruising the college campus checking out the girls. We were young, after all, in an ambulance, and despite the name on the side, they didn't know what a joke this company was or that the interview process consisted of stopping in and telling the manager I could start on Friday.

They didn't know the manager was a pervy old man with no skills or education, who solicited blow jobs from young girls new to the field, promising hours or raises in return. And they sure didn't know the plumber had to be called to unclog the toilets at the office, only to find the clog was caused by an obscene number of used condoms from all the after-hours sex going on. Despite the filth the name on the side of the truck represented, the star of life next to it did carry some clout, at least in our heads. But the girl chasing would have to wait. This morning we had to pick up a guy for a doctor's appointment.

We arrived early and kicked back in our seats to wait for a few minutes until we got a little closer to pick-up time. At five minutes 'til we pulled out our stretcher and walked up to the apartment. The door opened, and immediately I was met by an angry woman. "Where the hell have you been? His appointment is at 10:30!" she demanded.

"I know, ma'am. It's 9:55, and it's only seven minutes away."

"Whatever, y'all gon' be late."

I just shook my head, already irritated. Putting that aside, I redirected my attention to the patient. "Oh, you use oxygen?" I asked.

The woman chimed in again. "Yeah! He use' oxygen! You should know that!"

"Ma'am, I just met him for the first time in my life. There's no way that I could know that he uses oxygen, but it's not a big deal."

I sent my partner back out to get a tank, and she disappeared into the other room. I turned back to the patient and began talking to him again. Behind me, I heard a loud crash. I turned around to find she had put a full-sized mattress on top of my stretcher.

"He can't sit on that. Y'all gonna have to take him on that mattress."

I was baffled. I had never seen this before. I didn't know what to say.

"Ma'am, that isn't going to fit in the truck, and I can't seatbelt him on that thing. I can't take that," I tried to reason with this insane woman.

"Well, you gon' have to figure it out I guess, 'cause he can't sit on that."

Three strikes, I was done. In 911, you've got to deal with what you're given. In private service, you can refuse service, and today I exercised that ability for the first and only time in my career.

"Ma'am, you've been rude since I walked in the door, and this is ridiculous. I'm not taking him."

Her jaw dropped. "Whatchu mean you not gon' take him? How he gon' get to his appointment?"

"That's your problem now. Call someone else."

My partner had returned just in time to hear these words. He had no idea what was going on, and he didn't ask. He grabbed the head of the stretcher and helped me push it out, asking only once we were safely back in the truck and on the road. That is a true partner.

She's Gonna Be Thirsty

"Medic 64, Overdose."

That's a pretty common call in the hood. They're usually someone sleeping in their car or a heroin addict who has used a different dealer. Tonight dispatch felt compelled to let us know it was a child. My anxiety elevated. These sorts of calls always raise the heart rate and blood pressure. We can generally tell by the tone in the dispatcher's voice how serious the call will be, but on this night, I didn't detect she was worried. That's good. I calmed down a bit.

We arrived and received our second clue about the severity of the situation. When babies aren't breathing, someone runs them out to the truck. When babies are really sick, someone meets us at the street. I didn't see a baby, but there was a rather emphatic man standing at the curb flagging me down. My anxiety raised again. "Never let 'em see you sweat," I told myself.

I grabbed my bags and entered the residence where I found a dozen or more people sitting in the living room staring at me. There were a lot of kids, but I didn't see any that looked sick. "Who am I here for?" I asked, annoyed I had to ask. I was pointed to a little girl sitting on her grandmother's lap in the corner. She was shy and hid her face in grandma's shoulder, so I talked to grandma. "What happened?" I asked.

"I think she overdosed," Grandma explained.

"On what?"

"Salt."

"Uh, what? Like bath salts? Epsom salts? What kind of salt?" I pried further, irritated at the speed, or lack thereof, this conversation was progressing.

"Table salt." I stared back blankly. You can't be serious. My disgust must have been obvious because grandma finally began to use her words. "She gagged and then vomited."

"Well yeah, she ate pure salt. That's what you do when you get a mouth full of salt. How much did she eat?" I asked.

"About a teaspoon worth, but she threw most of it up!" she responded.

Again I shook my head. I couldn't handle this level of stupid. I didn't want to partake in this conversation anymore. "Do you want her to go to the hospital?" I asked, irritated.

"What are the long-term effects of eating that much salt?" she asked.

Do I really have to explain this to an old woman?

"She'll be thirsty," I replied sarcastically.

We have an acronym for this situation, DYD. It stands for "Damn, you dumb."

Sick Person

COVID was in full swing, and it was the middle of the day. Dispatch had alerted us to a "sick person." Sick person is sometimes the generic term for when a dispatcher doesn't really know how to categorize the call and just the words solicit irritated groans every time it comes over the air. These are the nausea, vomiting, diarrhea, drunk, bead in the nose, scratched by the cat, headache, fever, bit by a mosquito, stuffy nose, poison ivy rash, just won't eat, swallowed gum, etc. type of call.

Over the years, I have also learned these are the calls that can burn you if you get complacent. These calls have a tendency to go south in a hurry if you're not paying attention, and poor management or complacent assessment has cost many paramedics their careers, but most of the time, they are what they are. Today, there was not a lot to worry about. I was greeted by a young girl who led me into the house and sat down. I look around the room at who I presumed to be Mom, Dad, and daughter, and waited on someone to open the conversation, but they all just stared at me, saying nothing. Are you noticing a pattern here, dear reader?

"Who am I here for?" I asked. The girl spoke up and informed me she was the patient. "So what's going on?" I asked. She pulled off her sock and pointed to her toes. Nothing jumped out at me. "What?" I pressed further.

"My toenails are turning yellow!" she blurted out. "My grandma's toenails turned yellow, and I don't want my feet to look like hers!"

I looked to Mom, and then to Dad, as if to say, "Are you serious?" But they said nothing. They were invested and continued to stare at me expectantly, as if I was going to provide some miracle intervention to solve this problem right here and now. I tried really hard to be tactful, but there is really no way to tactfully explain to someone discolored toenails are not a medical emergency, are not a reason to call an ambulance, and there is nothing that can be done in the ER for it, but I did it, and I did it well.

Mom and Dad were suddenly in agreement with me. "That's what we told her!"

"And yet you let her call anyway," I muttered under my breath. What happened to parenting?

"So what can I do for it?"

Damned if I know. When I was going through lifesaving scenarios in paramedic school, somehow, this one failed to come up. I guess I should probably write a letter to someone about that or something.

Better Hurry Then

The Indiana winter dumped a foot of snow on the ground, and everything was delayed, including the private ambulance services. These are the services who transport patients to and from their doctor's appointments when they are unable to get there without assistance. I had just gotten to work and already I was picking up their slack.

I was familiar with the address. I had been there too many times for narcotic overdoses, but this morning, the notes simply read "sick person." I gave the obligatory groan and climbed the stairs to meet the patient who was up and walking around the apartment. She had packed a bag and had her shoes on. I guess this was a planned emergency. She directed me to grab her cell phone charger and cigarettes from the bedroom.

"Well before I do that, why don't you tell me why I'm here?" I asked.

"I got surgery this morning, and the ambulance company said they was gonna be late, so I need y'all to take me."

"Ma'am, can't you call a cab? This isn't what 911 is for," I tried to explain.

"Nah, I'm late, and ambulances get there faster," she retorted.

I was no longer annoyed, I was angry now.

"Ma'am, this isn't what ambulances are for, and there could be other emergencies that are more serious while you are occupying one of the very few ambulances in the city."

She was unmoved. "Well then we better get moving so you can get back faster," she said as she walked out the door. "Make sure you grab my cigarettes!"

It is for this type of call I feel EMS providers need to be made peace officers with citation issuing power. Maybe if selfishness had consequences, some of the abuses would stop.

I Feel Too Good

"I feel too good," said the elderly woman from her recliner. She was fully dressed and ready to go.

"What do you mean?" I asked, confused.

"Something ain't right. I feel too good and need to go to the hospital." I looked at my partner who appeared as baffled as I was, and then back to her. I attempted to clarify, thinking maybe she was having a stroke and was mixing up her words.

"I don't understand. Do you mean you feel bad?"

"NO! I usually feel like shit, but I feel good today. Something ain't right!"

"And you want to go to the hospital for that?" I asked, certain my question would stir some reason within this woman.

"Yep," she said, not taking the hint.

"And what do you want the hospital to do for you? Make you feel bad again?" I asked in one final attempt to display reason to a woman who clearly had none.

"I want them to figure out what's wrong with me! Something ain't right."

Alright, then, let's go, I guess. I radioed report to the hospital. "Medic 10 to hospital, we're enroute to you with a patient who has a chief complaint of... feeling too good."

There was a long pause on the frequency. "Come again, Medic 10?"

Fuck You, Cracker!

It was late, or maybe early. At this hour, I wasn't sure anymore. I hadn't had time to make my bed. The moon was full and the crazy juices, normally lurking just below the surface, had risen with the surging tides.

I responded to a call for an assault in a project neighborhood outside of my area. I walked into the apartment and was surprised to see several kids sitting in the front room. They were surprised to see me as well and let me know it. The cop pointed me to the bedroom where I found their mother, drunk and bleeding after being assaulted by her loving boyfriend. The kids followed me back. I attempted to assess her, but I couldn't hear over the heckling from these five- to twelve-year-olds.

"Get this white mother fucker outta here. Fuck you, cracker! You white devil."

Mom screamed at them, "Get the hell out!"

They left, and I resumed my questioning, but they returned a few moments later, adding to their jeers. It's a bit unsettling to be cussed out by a five-year-old or to meet one that is so focused on race. It's especially odd when you're used to being greeted by adoration and questions about your tools, trucks, and flashing lights from this age group, but for whatever reason, they didn't like me in their house. They were focused more on hating me than they were on their mother's condition. This level of apathy tells me they are well accustomed to both a drunk mom and the violence that required my presence this evening. This level of anger toward me reflects the parenting, but I suppose I shouldn't expect parent of the year attributes from a woman whose children are awake in the middle of the night on a school night.

This experience was not ordinary, but it wasn't all that unique either. This is the only time I have experienced young kids that are so brazen and indoctrinated in hatred, but from the adults, it comes much more frequently. There have been several occasions where my patients refused to allow me to treat them because I was white and demanded my Black partner be the one to do so. I explained to them they required advanced intervention, and I was the only qualified provider on scene, but they didn't care. They wanted the Black guy.

I've seen this go the other way as well, particularly with older white people toward Black providers, or with men toward women. I am aware this goes in all directions, but prior to this moment, it was not something I had personally experienced, and it was quite shocking to this suburban boy.

DNR

"Cardiac Arrest. Engine 10, Respond." We had been given our marching orders, and we recognized the address. This man was a chronically ill patient with a short temper and a bad affect. To put it simply, he was a jerk. We had been here many times before. As a matter of fact, we had already been here once today. He turned us away. His mother was worried he had been skipping dialysis, and for good reason. He hadn't gone in five days, which was pushing the limits of what the body can tolerate.

Earlier, we had explained if he didn't go with us, he would likely die. He didn't care, which is not altogether uncommon with the chronically ill. People just get tired of the fight, and at some point, resign themselves to the inevitable. Most express it well. This man, however, did so in his usual manner. "Man, shut the fuck up and get out of my house."

"Whatever. Your choice, my man." There was nothing we could do there, so we left.

Later that evening, our warnings played out. He was dead. With a Do Not Resuscitate (DNR) order in place, and the fact he had stopped life sustaining treatment that ultimately led to his death, there was nothing I could do, nor was I permitted to by law if I could. His mother attempted to revoke the DNR order, but this was not her legal right. We tried to explain these orders are put in place by the physician and the patient, and we intended to honor his wishes. We declined her request for revocation, and she unleashed an onslaught of racist slurs.

According to her, we just didn't want to help him because we were "white supremacists who hate Black people." Captain Boz sent us out of the house and weathered the brunt of the attack by himself. This sort of thing is exhausting, but I don't usually take it personally. In this case, I chalked it up to the irrationality of a grieving mother. That is until after the death of my own son. After that I realized even though everyone grieves differently, grief doesn't have to make you unkind. This is one of the many things that drove me to search for inner peace outside of that city.

I've Got No Pulse

Some requests defy all logic and reasoning. It was a split scene, and initially, there was some confusion about who the patient was. At the first scene I came to, there was a man sitting on the curb in handcuffs. The officer explained he had beaten up his wife down the road. They called us because her mother had chased him down and tackled him to the ground, where she held him until police arrived.

"Are you hurt?" I asked him. He shook his head no. "So you don't need EMS?"

"Nah, take me to jail. Fuck y'all, and fuck these racist ass cops!"

That was good enough for me. We got back into the ambulance and were alerted to a second patient at a different location—his wife. We cleared the scene and proceeded to her. Her eye was swollen shut and the size of a softball. I was very concerned about the possibility of facial fractures or other injuries, but she was adamant she didn't want to go to the hospital. I explained I was concerned the swelling was putting pressure on the vasculature and the optic nerve behind her eye and failure to be seen by a doctor could result in the loss of her vision.

My medical knowledge meant absolutely nothing against her drunk wisdom. She disagreed and decided she would be fine. Now frustrated, I got a doctor on the line, hoping he would be able to relay my concerns in a different way and convince her to be transported, but again, she knew better and declined treatment or transport. Having exhausted all means at my disposal to get her to do what was best for herself, I had her sign the form and started to clear from this scene as well.

Just as I closed the door of the ambulance, one of the officers started waving at me and alerted me the man at the other location now stated he didn't have a pulse.

"He does or the officer with him does?" I attempted to clarify.

"He does."

I didn't need to evaluate him to determine that wasn't true.

I returned to the original scene and found him sitting on the curb in handcuffs again. "Do you need EMS?" I asked.

"Yeah, my heart is stopping."

I quickly checked his pulse, and again, found it to be normal. "Your pulse is normal," I informed him.

"Well, I got a heart condition," he replied.

"I assume the heart condition pre-exists this moment, so why do you need to go to the hospital now?" I asked.

"For my heart condition," he answered defiantly.

"What is your heart condition?"

He referenced a blood pressure problem, which for the moment was also fine, so I asked again, "Why do you need to go to the hospital?"

"Because that's where I want to go."

Ah, got it. He just wanted to be a thorn in everyone's side and avoid jail for a while longer.

Those are some of the more egregious examples, but after all these years, I could literally fill this book with these stories, and it is not limited to the public. Cops are notorious for dumping drunk people on EMS because it is easier than having to process them into jail—not that jail is the most appropriate place for them either. Nursing homes are some of the worst offenders of patient dumping, especially when their patient loads exceed their staffing capabilities or when a patient just becomes a major time suck for them. They also don't like to wait for the appropriate service to solve their problem, so they call 911 for things like abnormal blood work because they know there is no wait.

While the often-hostile attitudes are frustrating, I would not cite them as a core reason for my growing agitation, at first. It was easy to overlook as pure ignorance. I knew I was doing right by them and hoped one day they would see that too. The most consequential reason I burnt out was the overwhelming load of absolute nonsense I responded to with regularity.

Good medics live for the calls they can be useful. The vast majority of the ambulance using population views it as a taxi to be used as they see fit, and the emergency room is their primary care point. One of the things that is unique to underserved communities is the reliance on the hospital for literally everything. From toothaches to management of chronic pain, food provision or just a place to sleep for the night, bridging medication gaps and avoiding jail, they utilize the most expensive form of healthcare for it all.

As a paramedic, I have one option, to take them. When a community is suffering from poverty, they have difficult decisions to make. Preventative care is nonexistent because many providers don't accept low-income insurance and they require payment at the time of service. The ER doesn't require payment at all, nor does an ambulance, and when they get the bill, I've had patients tell me they don't care what it is going to cost because they're not going to pay it anyway. I admire the honesty, if not the defiance.

When you must decide whether to eat or take a blood pressure medication, guess what takes the back seat? "I'll be fine without that medication. I didn't even feel sick when the doctor told me to start taking it." They call high blood pressure the silent killer. It kills your kidneys, damages your heart, and increases the risk of heart attacks and strokes, among other things. Healthy food is more expensive than burgers and chicken nuggets from the local fast-food joint or virtually anything out of a box, so obesity becomes a problem, which leads to diabetes, liver problems, and heart disease.

Add in the problems of alcoholism, drug dependence, and violence that plague impoverished communities and you end up with a very sick population generating a lot of calls, and I haven't even talked about the call volume from the people this chapter is about, the selfish and dumb. It is maddening to know all these problems, understand the causes, have ideas to resolve them, and have only one option at our disposal—the hospital. All the while, every one of us knows there are better and more holistic solutions. We don't mind being busy. If you need us and we can do something to make your situation better, that is the lifeblood that keeps us going, but the one thing that infuriates us all is having our time wasted by somebody who is either too stupid to know better or too selfish to care.

Throughout my career, there have been days where I have run all day and never even used my stretcher. Everyone got the bench seat, which is reserved for those deemed not worth the effort of cleaning the stretcher. I had form narratives on my computer and would just copy and paste it for the specific call type, changing the age, sex, and whatever small detail deviated from the standard. I gave them titles like "drunk-cops can't take to jail" or "toe pain." Some of these calls are so far out there though, there is no pre-written narrative that could adequately describe the stupid human in front of me.

For a while, I was convinced these sorts of scenarios would end if we could just get people to understand what is and isn't an emergency. I was still convinced people were generally intelligent and good, and they had just been conditioned to think 911 was something it wasn't. I talked about public education campaigns and purchasing billboards to set the record straight. I considered requesting airtime on local news stations or having conversations with doctors about using EMS in a more educative way. As I said, I was an idealist, but none of those things ever came to fruition. Then something happened that changed my view entirely.

The Coronavirus arrived on our doorstep. Overnight our call volume dwindled to a trickle. People were scared to death to go to the hospital for fear they might contract the deadly virus, so they didn't. They didn't call except when it was an absolute emergency, and sometimes not even then. Doctors recognized the value of keeping them home, so they outlined protocols for what should and shouldn't be transported and trusted paramedics to make that decision, a novel idea. For the first time in my career, I was allowed to refuse transport or make recommendations about home care or more appropriate options. It was a healthcare system that worked, that made sense, that was utilizing resources appropriately. It was a magical time in EMS.

For all those nonsense complaints I talked about above, I only refused transport one time in the month I was allowed to. Those calls just weren't coming in anymore. I spent more time trying to convince people who needed to go that their fear of death in a hospital was less justified than the reality they might actually die from the emergency they called about if they didn't go. I was elated at first, and then incensed.

People had proven they knew what an emergency was all this time, and they just didn't care. They had proven they could handle their own problems without my intervention, and they just didn't want to. Doctors had admitted EMS could be trusted to make wise medical decisions with limited oversight, and then took it away as fast as they could because something interesting happened. The hospitals who were so worried about being overrun were dead.

There was a night where one of the busier local hospitals had only had one patient in the ER for the entire night. Discussions about the inability to pay staff and layoffs began. Nurses were sent home for low census, and hospital administrators worried they might have to close their doors. The pendulum had swung so far in the opposite direction, it simply wasn't sustainable, so we just stopped. We resumed operations as usual, and as the pandemic dragged on, the fear waned, and people resumed business as usual. The difference was now I had the knowledge they knew what an ambulance and an ER were for, and they just didn't care.

If you want to talk about ways to kick burnout into overdrive, this is a prime case study. Previously, I could chalk it up to ignorance. Now I had to attribute it to pure selfishness. It became abundantly clear medicine was about the Benjamins—a contract built on the depravity of the system and those who abuse it. The victim? The American taxpayer, the *actual* sick patient, and the low-level provider. My idealism was dead.

CHAPTER 12

THE EFFECT OF COVID

In January 2020, I remember reading a friend's post on Facebook. "OMG, people. Coronavirus is just a COLD! Stop freaking out!" This was the first time I had heard of this exotic illness, and I didn't pay it much mind. I'm old enough to remember H1N1 and Ebola. Neither event had produced what was promised, at least in my world. They faded as fast as they came, and that is what I expected of the Coronavirus as well. In fact, I was almost certain it was 100 percent political, and I commented as much on a YouTube video about how this was going to fundamentally reshape the world as we knew it. "Give me a break, the election will end, and in 2 months, we will have forgotten the word 'COVID.'"

In retrospect, this puts me in the company of great names such a Daryl Zanuck who said in 1946, "Television won't be able to hold on to any market that it captures after the first six months. People will soon get tired of staring at a plywood box every night." Or Ken Olsen when he said in 1977, "There is no reason anyone would want a computer in their home."

We read this now on our MacBook and iPhone while watching our 75" flat screen TV and laugh at them, wondering how they could be so shortsighted. But then, hindsight *is* 20/20 after all. How does one understand a pandemic if they have never experienced one? The known commodity was hyperbole and fearmongering, and this felt just like all those other times.

In February 2020, I began to hear rumblings about COVID-19, but I still wasn't paying attention. I tuned out politicians calling Donald Trump xenophobic for banning travel from China as they trotted down the streets of Chinatown and invited their constituents to gather because there was nothing to fear. You know, business as usual. This only served to confirm my suspicions this was politically motivated.

On February 17, 2020, my partner left for vacation. That week I had three respiratory cases of unexplainable origin. They exhibited shortness of breath, low oxygen levels, and clear lung sounds with no other symptoms. This presentation is consistent with pulmonary embolism, but as I would learn, was also consistent with COVID-19. I treated these patients unmasked, using aerosolizing procedures, which we now know is a good way to give the virus a ride from your nose to mine, and I thought nothing more of it.

When my partner returned, I told her, "You know, I had three pulmonary embolisms while you were gone. It was the weirdest thing."

"That *is* weird," she remarked.

I feel confident now these were undiagnosed COVID cases. Around the same time, my wife, supervising a student clinical rotation in the hospital, remarked about how sad it was that a patient she had, who was in the hospital following back surgery, had spiked a fever and deteriorated quickly. He ultimately died, which we learned about while visiting my family in Tennessee. They had tested him for nearly everything but came up short. A month later, they did a post-mortem COVID test and confirmed it was in fact the cause of death. She had been unmasked in the room for hours.

On March 6, 2020, Indiana confirmed its first official COVID case. Masks and hand sanitizer were in short supply, and Dr. Anthony Fauci began his media parade and begged people to stop purchasing them because it was much more important for healthcare providers to be able to have that supply. Faced with the shortage, within a week, my department purchased P-100 respirators that were supposed to protect us against all forms of particulates, including COVID-19, and established a policy that it was to be worn on every call. When we were finished, we were to put on a surgical mask and wear it in the truck with each other and while at the station. They shut down entrances to the fire station to "reduce germ spread," banned the public and workers from entering the stations, required sanitization of all surfaces twice daily, bought "foggers" to sanitize the trucks following each call, and placed bleach rags by the doors for us to sanitize our boots as we entered from the field.

We had no idea what we were dealing with. It was droplet; no it was airborne. No, still droplet, but it lived forever on surfaces. No, it didn't live on these surfaces, but you should probably sanitize your groceries and leave them outside for a while before bringing them in. There was so much everchanging and conflicting information, that none of us knew what to think or believe. Who could fault them for the abundance of caution? But for my good or not, this avalanche of changes began to play games with my mind.

In late March, I went to the grocery store, and as I walked down the aisles, I could feel my heart rate rising and my cheeks and chest started to burn. "What is going on?" I asked myself. Then I realized I was subconsciously holding my breath, and I had begun to see the people around me as walking incubators for this unknown virus. I forced myself to breathe. I made it my singular focus, to the point where I began to hyperventilate. I left the crowded aisle I was standing in and decided I would come back for that item.

But as I walked from aisle to aisle, there were people everywhere, and I couldn't escape or place enough distance between myself and them. Soon I was having a full-blown panic attack, the first I had ever had. So I left my cart in the middle of the aisle and walked out of the store empty handed. I was on the front lines, dealing with it every day, and yet in such a short time, I had become so dependent upon the barrier the P-100 provided that when facing the world without it, I felt vulnerable.

Not long after the first case arrived in the cornfields of Indiana, I had my first known encounter with it. It finally felt real. It was a young man who had been quarantined for a few days, and his sister became concerned when she was unable to reach him. She met us outside and informed us he was COVID positive. We reacted in a manner more appropriate for a nuclear meltdown.

We ran back to the truck and donned our gowns, goggles, gloves, and face shields, the official uniform of COVID-19. We were already wearing the masks and wandered in looking like Stay Puff Marshmallow men. It was a false alarm. He was just asleep and hadn't heard her knocking. With no patient to take care of, we began the arduous process of removing the PPE as we were taught— break the gown and peel it off, sanitize your gloves, roll the gloves off one at a time (rolling the second one over the first one into a little ball), throw it away, sanitize your hands, remove the mask, take off the glasses, sanitize your hands, disinfect with Lysol, shower, change clothes, wash the dirty ones, and fog the ambulance. It was exhausting, and it was constant, and in retrospect, it was unnecessary. Every time we suspected the patient was positive, we went through this process, day after day, call after call.

When I was a high-rise window washer, the first time I descended from a building, I was paralyzed with fear. I did my best to clean the windows without leaving the safety bubble of the two-foot lift, but the thing is, windows are larger than two feet, and if I was going to do a separate drop every two feet, it would take so long I would have to start over again by the time I was done. That job required I get brave. My boss yelled down to me, "Lean out and get it!"

At first I was hesitant and only stuck my arm out, which broadened my reach by three feet to either side, but I still wasn't very effective. As I grew more accustomed to the height and began to trust the equipment, I got more adventurous and leaned out a bit more, and then a bit more, until I was hanging off the edge of the lift struggling to get a corner I just couldn't quite reach. This is a metaphor for how I felt about COVID.

Fear of the unknown initially paralyzed me. We didn't know anything at first, but over time, as we gained knowledge and more studies came out, COVID transitioned from a pandemic to a nuisance. The PPE was hampering my ability to do my job. I quit bothering with the gowns except on the rare occasion I needed to get up close and personal with a patient. My job is mostly to direct others and make decisions. I was rarely involved in patient movement or physical procedures. I also questioned the purpose of wearing a gown when I had to change clothes anyway. It seemed pointless.

My respirator caused its own problems. If you've ever worn a P-100, you may be able to relate. My voice echoed inside the plastic and rubber contraption and muffled my speech. I could have auditioned for the role of Charlie Brown's teacher. I constantly had to repeat myself and found I was always pulling it down so my patients could understand me, thereby rendering it pointless. The alternative was to give up on my line of questioning out of frustration and sit quietly, making assumptions based upon what I could see, which wasn't much.

My peripheral vision was gone because the filters blocked my line of sight. I found myself tripping over things constantly. It also seemed to direct sound around my ears, so I caught myself turning my head to hear people's responses even when I wasn't wearing the stupid thing. I found procedures, such as starting IVs, difficult because of the visual obstruction and the fact I had to drive it into my chest in order to get a decent angle to be able to see what I was doing. And if all of that wasn't enough, they're uncomfortable!

Good assessment requires the use of your nose. The mask did nothing to seal out the smell of weed and garbage funk, but it sure did a lot to inhibit my ability to detect alcohol or the subtle, fruity smell of ketones emanating from patients in diabetic ketoacidosis. Decubitus ulcers, c-diff, GI bleeds, and urinary tract infections all have a distinct odor that were very difficult to pick up. It's hard to be a good paramedic when you can't see, hear, speak, breathe, or smell and have a persistent headache from the pressure it placed on the sinuses. Do you know how hard it is to think through problems when you can't think about anything else but the plastic muzzle on your face?

The masks also presented a problem in relating to other human beings. People expect reassurance and comfort from us during scary times, but I just couldn't get there with this contraption on my face. Facial expressions are important when expressing empathy, confidence, competence, and reassurance. One of the hallmarks of my skillset is my ability to communicate and relate to patients on a personal level, but when you take the human element a face provides out of the equation, I was nothing more than a robot yelling technical terms at confused and scared people who couldn't understand me anyway.

After months of this, I was done. I wasn't scared anymore. I was convinced that if I hadn't caught it yet, I wasn't going to catch it. If I was going to catch it, then let it come, and let's get it over with. The departmental policies on masking did not reflect my level of apathy. In fact, they didn't reflect the hospital preferences either. It became clear that P-100s were there as a lawsuit inhibitor, but they did nothing to protect our patients as there was an exhalation valve. It protected me, who had a miniscule chance of death due to my age and lack of pre-existing conditions, but not the little old lady in the nursing home who had a very real chance of dying should she catch the illness.

Because of this, hospitals insisted we switch to a surgical mask prior to bringing patients in, but the department persisted in enforcing the policy. "If you get COVID, it's your own fault because our policies have proven so effective that no COVID case can be traced back to the workplace." That statement came out of the face of a fully grown, supposedly intelligent, human adult with a golden badge. How do you argue with reason like that? I voiced my concerns to my supervisor and asked when we could switch to a basic surgical mask. He forwarded it up the chain, and they passed the ball around to avoid making any decision on the matter.

They continued to insist we wear the P-100 on every call and the surgical mask any time we were riding in the truck with our partners. They disciplined an officer for his subordinates not wearing one in a truck or while at the station, even when he wasn't working that day, and they sent a few people home for failing to do so. This meant, some days, I was in a mask for eighteen to twenty hours.

Finally, in February 2021, the chief decided to pay a visit to the stations. I had worked there for over a year, and it was the first time I had seen him. I was told if I had concerns, to be respectful but to voice them, as there was no way he could know if nobody spoke up. I took that to heart.

"How are things going in the EMS world?" he asked.

I laughed. "Well, Chief, I've never been more unhappy in my career," I said.

He looked stunned at the admission, and the deputy chief burst out in laughter, probably out of sheer shock I would be so brazen with the big man. He shifted in his chair nervously. I was honestly at a point where I just didn't care and needed someone to know how I felt. Don't ask questions you don't want the answers to.

"Really?" he exclaimed. "Tell me why."

Holding up a gaiter mask, effectively as thin as panty hose, I said, "This right here. I'm vaccinated, and there's no science behind this. The largest study done to date on masking says there is no evidence this provides any level of added protection. A Danish study of 3,000 participants, half of which were masked, the other half were not, showed a 0.2 percent difference in contraction rate between the two control groups. As a result, they concluded they could not advise a mask mandate."

He tried to wiggle off the hook. "Well we're trying to do the best we can for our people and keep you guys from getting sick. We can't make changes while the CDC is still recommending masks."

"That's exactly the problem chief. Everybody is scared to be the first man through the wall. This will never change because nobody wants to risk being the one that changes it."

He pondered for a moment. "Well do you think a local fire chief is going to have any influence on the people in charge?" he asked smugly, no doubt feeling like he got me.

"No, but you are the chief of *this* department. You have the authority to make changes to *this* department," I retorted. *Holy shit,* I thought. *Did I just become Boz?* I checked my lip for a mustache, but found it as bare as a baby's butt.

"So what do you want to see done?" he asked.

I rattled my response off so quickly I am sure it sounded rehearsed. I probably had rehearsed it a dozen times in my grumblings with coworkers. "I am burnt out. I'm tired. COVID has taken its toll on me. Every interaction is a high stress interaction. My days off are spent sleeping and recovering from this insane call volume. Every time I go out the door, I worry that one of your spies is going to rat me out for breathing fresh air, and I'm going to get written up. I want to have the autonomy to decide when a P-100 is necessary. I want this mask nonsense around the station and in the trucks to end, and frankly, I need more time off. I've been here a year and only get one day off this year. I'm taking it in October."

Not wanting to spend any more time on this, he simply replied, "Let me have the EMS Chief take a look at this, and he'll schedule a private meeting with you to follow up."

That never happened. What did happen was a "change" to the masking policy that basically just said the same thing as before. The only difference was the P-100 masks no longer had to be worn outside of the patient compartment of the ambulance except during the initial interaction. That benefited the firefighters who were never in the patient compartment, but it did nothing for me.

A few days later, they sent me an invite to a virtual mental health conference, and that was the extent of their "give a damn." I made the personal decision that because I was vaccinated, I was going to wear a surgical mask for the run of the mill patient and stop wearing the P-100, and I was not going to wear the mask anymore while riding down the road with my partner, who was also vaccinated. "Write me up if you have to," I decided.

My attitude may have sucked, but I was choosing my mental health and sanity over arbitrary, nonscientific policy. And you know what? It took me *three* years to finally contract the virus=. I didn't have to ride dirty for too much longer though. The CDC finally released their very obvious and delayed findings the scientific community knew all along. Vaccinated people weren't spreaders, at least prior to the Delta variant. Finally, the department made the mask policy reflect common sense—mostly.

There were other effects of COVID I don't feel were given enough weight. In fact, it is my opinion very little decision making during the pandemic reflected common sense. One of the things I found most disheartening was the lack of family involvement with loved ones. We were taking dementia patients to the hospital who had no knowledge of their health history, why I was there, who the strange man was that was kidnapping them, or even where they lived, and sending them to be seen by doctors who diagnosed and treated based on what I could relay to them from my fifteen-minute interaction with the family. They were then sent home with no explanation to the family of their findings, who called us back because nothing had changed since they had last seen them.

On one occasion, I responded to a man with an altered mental status. His wife was in despair because he had just returned home that afternoon after a four month stay in a nursing home where she'd had no contact with him because he was unable to speak and she wasn't allowed into the facility. She was thankful to finally have him home, but she was beside herself because he could speak when he left, and nobody had relayed that he had lost that ability to her. Now he was mute, and she didn't know anything about him.

She had no idea how to take care of the various tubes protruding from his body or what any of them were for. She had received no direction, no home health, nothing. We did our best to comfort her, but the situation was so beyond understanding that I didn't know what to say. She was obviously emotional and worried she was sending him off to hear nothing again for months longer. This situation wasn't unique. Every time I closed the door of my ambulance, I did so knowing this may have been the last time a family would see their loved one. I grew tired of explaining to family that visitors were not allowed in the hospital.

On the other side of things, nursing home residents were completely isolated. Many nursing and senior living facilities had policies that restricted residents from leaving their rooms, even with a mask, and prohibited them from even going to the grocery store or to run other errands. If they did so, they were required to quarantine elsewhere for two weeks prior to being allowed to return. This sort of thing went on for months, and I visited more distraught, depressed elderly folks than I ever cared to.

Mental health took a dive during the pandemic, and I honestly don't see the purpose. If nurses could leave, go to the grocery store, be with their families, and then return to work while masked, why couldn't a family member? Instead, the elderly spent Thanksgiving and Christmas alone while politicians put out public service announcements stating, "If you want to see Grandma next Thanksgiving, maybe skip this one." It was appalling.

Outside the nursing homes, we were seeing people that were terrified to leave their homes. They'd been vaccinated and were still wearing masks but wouldn't leave even after a year in total isolation. Two years of a twenty-four-hour news cycle keeping the fear volume on ten really did a number on these folks. It was sad. It really infuriated me. I am seeing red even as I write this, and we can point the finger at the healthcare establishment for allowing it to happen just as much as the politicians who kept the fear drum beating and the media echo chamber who reinforced it. I'm mad at all of them, but most of all healthcare practitioners and administrators.

We knew better. We are trained scientific-minded individuals who should have been leading by example. Instead we posted cutesy banners on our Facebook profiles. "I can't stay home, I'm a nurse." "I can't stay home, I'm essential." Somehow our egos became so inflated we completely forgot about the whole person. For a year the only trainings I received were on COVID updates. For a year I facilitated the separation of families, and nurses and doctors stood by while people died alone and without a familiar face around them. For a year we told people this virus with a 99.5 percent survival rate was far more dangerous than the desperation they were feeling from the isolation. For a year, we allowed politics to dictate healthcare policy and not science, and every day that goes by, it becomes more and more evident just how deeply the slimy tentacles of politics have infiltrated the healthcare industry.

I have spent a career pursuing evidence-based education and methodology and in a single year, it was completely wiped away in favor of politics. You may disagree, but I believe the only reason in May 2021 we were still not open as a country, why we were vaccinated and still wearing masks, and why kids were still not in schools full time was because if the political class could keep us scared and keep us believing death was lurking just around the corner, then they could pass massive spending bills full of unpopular political wish lists disguised as pandemic relief, and they threw us a few hundred bucks to look the other way.

The COVID crisis has been a roller coaster, and I don't want to discount it one bit because I know how deadly it could be for certain segments of the population, but the second the populous was vaccinated, or at least available to everyone who wanted to be, we should have gone back to normal. Instead, we continued to flounder, and in some cases, even ramped up the restrictions and precautions.

Did anyone calculate the toll the isolation took on kids? These were kids who needed to be active in sports and extracurriculars, who were establishing relationships that would carry them through their high school years, and in some cases, the rest of their lives. They needed social interaction with their peers to develop and mature emotionally. They needed interaction to cure the terrible loneliness they were experiencing.

Suicide rates for teens went through the roof. At Riley Children's Hospital in Indianapolis, the month of October 2020 saw a 250 percent increase in suicide attempts over October 2019. For the year, the total was up to 108 from sixty-seven in the previous year. Benioff Children's Hospital in Oakland, California reported similar findings. I saw the intense anxiety in my twelve-year old as she returned to school part time for the first time in almost two years. Being new to the district, she sat by herself at lunch for several weeks before finally making a friend and inserting herself into a lunch group. Her anxiety began to lift a bit but returned months later when schools voted to return full time.

I was confused, and when I asked her why she was so nervous, she said "It's kind of like the first day again, Dad. I still haven't met half of my class." She had been on a blue/red schedule with students being grouped in one or the other, and she was right. I had never even considered that. She adapted but not every kid did.

I transported more than my fair share of kids with suicidal feelings, who attempted, or worse, succeeded in those years. The worst case I dealt with was a teenager with a self-inflicted gunshot wound to the head. My stomach is gone for holding the shattered skull fragments of a child together as the brain matter leaks out around my gloves. I'm sorry for the graphic image, but the description is intentional.

We can sweep all of this under the rug under the guise of safety and public health emergency, but I can't hide from that image, and I don't want anybody else to be able to either. I see that kid's face daily and can't help but think this was avoidable if only we had listened to the science that told us kids were not vectors for spreading the illness, that kids were at a nearly zero risk of death or serious injury from the virus, and that *this* public health crisis was the real boogie man for this age group. Health is not one size fits all. We devoted all our attention to one issue and ignored the consequences our decisions created.

As the days have gone on, the health crisis within the health crisis hasn't gotten better. In fact, it's gotten far worse. The dominoes are falling and taking down everything around them. I received a report from my employer a few weeks ago that noted our call volume had increased three times over the same period in

2020 at the height of the pandemic. Local media outlets are releasing daily reports about overcrowding in the ERs and ICUs and often talking about how it is not *just* because of COVID.

Anecdotally, that is consistent with what I am seeing. That may even over-state it a bit. It should say "while COVID contributes very little to these numbers." Indiana noted an increase in EMS calls from 750,000 in 2019 to over a million in 2020, and it hasn't seemed to slow down. We're doing more with less. Burnt out providers are simply walking off the job, and nobody is replacing them, but the calls keep coming. If not COVID, what is behind the rise in people seeking medical attention? Unwarranted calls for service certainly contribute to those numbers, but they're not responsible for all of them.

Over the last couple of years, I have noted a rise in high acuity patients. These are folks having heart attacks, strokes, respiratory difficulties, or other issues that require a lot of skilled hands-on care. I've asked my peers and doctors what they think is behind this. The answer I get most often is shrugging shoulders. An-other common response is, "Lack of preventative care for a year." But I don't think that's it either. People weren't exactly consistent with mammograms, dental clean-ings, and colonoscopies before the pandemic, so I don't think taking a year away from them caused this level of sickness. I have my own theory.

I believe it was the constant pump of unadulterated stress and fear mon-gering into our society, coupled with people not working, not participating in recre-ation, and having nothing better to do than surf social media and watch sensationalist news networks during the lockdowns. Beyond that, in their private interactions, they discussed the elephant in the room with everyone who would listen. COVID is all people talked about. Their theories, their worries, their frus-trations, their anger toward others, their opinions on the vaccines and on masks. Anything and everything. Their employers were closed, so they worried about where their next meal would come from, or if they would be able to make their house payment next month, and so on and so forth.

Beyond the pandemic, we had a year of rioting and tense apprehension every time there was a report of an unarmed person of color being shot by police, a bitter election, arguments about the integrity of that election, and, subsequently, insurrection in Washington, a political class who couldn't get along, and a public health agency who did not seem to be able to decide if it was a science agency or a political agency. For those of us who were still working, there was no place to decompress. You couldn't go on vacation, to the movies, to a baseball game, or anywhere we once went to blow off steam. For almost two years, and arguably for a decade before that, we have been sitting in a pool of tension and stress, and all this combined led to a rise in disease. Let me give you the quick down and dirty.

Stress causes cortisol and epinephrine levels to rise. These are the hormones the body releases that allow us to be able to function during periods of high stress. This is a good thing in small doses, but prolonged exposure to cortisol is well documented to cause increases in harmful body fat, blood sugar, blood pressure, and inflammation within the body. This is causing us to develop high blood pressure, diabetes, and obesity, all of which are risk factors for stroke, heart disease, and kidney failure. Stress is literally killing us and, the faucet, AKA the news media and political class, dumping the stress into our lives are stuck open. Again, this is just a theory, but I believe the lens of history will confirm my suspicions as doctors investigate this phenomenon further.

Chapter 13

Cinderella Syndrome

There is a huge disparity between what people think EMS does and what EMS actually does. If I had a nickel for every time I was called an "ambulance driver," I'd be a wealthy man. Ambulance driver is a four letter word many providers find particularly derogatory since it diminishes our skillset to taxi driver status.

Over the years, I have had numerous arguments in the back of an ambulance with irate patients who became upset after the ambulance didn't immediately start moving after loading them. "Let's go! What are we waiting on?" they demand. People are often unaware there is little difference between what I do and what initial care in the emergency room looks like, and that earlier intervention is to their benefit. I think this fact is sometimes lost on our doctor and nurse peers in the emergency department as well.

There has been some effort to bridge that understanding by having physicians, and occasionally nurses, do a short rotation in the field while in their residency or new hire training, but this is on a limited case by case basis. Each time I have had them with me though, they have remarked about how similar our assessment is to that of their own and marveled at the autonomous decision making and treatment capabilities we possess.

Even more so than the ambulance driver label, the lack of understanding of the differences between an EMT and a paramedic grate on my nerves. I honestly don't know why. I don't know how I could expect the lay person to know the difference, but perhaps it is because I have had to explain this to my own family repeatedly, and they still look at me like I have two heads and tell me about how they tell everyone they know their son is an EMT. I just shake my head.

I think people think EMT is the politically correct term for paramedics, like sanitary engineer is for garbage man or custodial worker is for janitor. Perhaps they just think they can be used interchangeably, and in a sense they can. Afterall, there is no way they can know the certification level of the person that shows up. All paramedics are EMTs, but not all EMTs are paramedics. By now you're probably thinking, "Dude it's just a title." You're right, and I promise my ego is not that fragile.

I have worked with the "nurses can't do anything without a doctor's permission" types, or the ones that spend hours lamenting how they do the same job a doctor does for an eighth of the pay. I'm not that guy and those things are far from true. I am less bothered by the title than the lack of understanding of the knowledge and skills behind the title. I think if people understood what they were getting when they called 911, they would be much more inclined to demand better service and support pay increases and additional staffing. I think if doctors understood our training, they would be more likely to expand our scope of practice. And if leadership understood the job we are doing, they would stop asking us to do more with less and go to the carpet to lobby on our behalf. In pursuit of these ends, I think now is a good time to explain the differences.

EMT school lasts between two weeks, in an accelerated program, to six months under normal circumstances and is around 170 hours of training. In that program they will learn to assess patients for life threatening injuries or medical conditions, stop bleeding, administer a limited number of medications, and to do CPR and deliver ventilations if your heart or breathing stops. These are the basics of lifesaving and the foundation for all things EMS. EMTs are vital to the system. The saying is paramedics save patients, but EMTs save paramedics, because as we become more advanced, it's easy to overlook the basics and jump straight to the more advanced stuff.

Paramedic school is a bit more intensive and usually takes eighteen to twenty-four months to complete. This training takes around 1800 hours of classroom time and 300 to 400 hours of internship training. In some cases, the paramedic will graduate with an associate degree in emergency medical services. We learn much more about the body and the chemistry that makes it all work together, various drugs and how they interact, advanced assessment skills, cardiology, and so much more.

Would you be surprised to learn that when your heart stops beating, the drugs, procedures, and treatments you will receive are the same on the floor of your home as they are in a sterile hospital room? Would it shock you to learn the Advanced Cardiac Life Support algorithms do not vary on either end of the ambulance? Or while those procedures are developed in university laboratories and hospitals by research scientists and medical doctors, in many cases, the doctors and nurses in the ER have learned them from a paramedic who taught the class? Did you know if your heart slows down, I can speed it up, or if it speeds up, I can slow it down?

If your airway becomes obstructed, I can cut a hole in your trachea and insert a breathing tube, and if you have a collapsed lung, I can insert a needle into your chest to ease your breathing. If they fill with fluid, I can use a special pressurized mask to promote air exchange, and if they become restricted, as they do with asthma or other pulmonary ailments, I can give you medications that will open them up. If you're having a baby, I can deliver it, and if you get into a car accident with that baby and you don't survive, I can perform emergency surgery to remove the baby in hopes of salvaging at least one life out of the tragedy. If you didn't know, you're not alone. Most don't know until they need us to do one of these things.

In the last chapter, I talked about the effects of COVID and administrative indifference, and I cannot think of a more perfect example to discuss in this chapter. Several months into the pandemic, when things were beginning to slow down a bit, my department issued a small bonus as a "thank you." There was only one problem. It wasn't allocated for the EMS providers! That's right. Us. The ones stuck in the back of the ambulance with the sick, day in and day out, were excluded. It was only after the firefighter union president went to the trustee and demanded we be included and recognized for our efforts that the check was cut.

But it didn't matter, the damage was done. It showed us exactly how little they thought of us. As far as I was concerned, they could keep their money. After taxes, it was a joke anyway. I'd rather have had a day off. Municipalities around us also received bonuses, but there was one jurisdiction that issued perhaps the most insulting "thank you" of all—a voucher for free candy at a movie theatre. Wow, what a prize.

As much of a slap in the face as those "thank yous" were, we're kind of used to them. If you're in EMS, you've become a bit of a connoisseur of the proverbial fecal sandwich. We don't mind the smell so much anymore, and after a while, the taste doesn't bother you like it used to either. It's the sheer number of them we are served that gets old. When you eat the same thing day in and day out, you find ways to spice it up, but even with a little salt and hot sauce, sometimes you just get tired of being expected to smile and say thank you when they plop it on your plate.

Let me paint a picture with the facts. Did you know the average salary for an EMT is $36,650 per year, and for a paramedic, it only increases to $38,820 per year? For a police officer, that number rises to $53,200, and for a firefighter, it's $51,119. However, paramedicine is the only profession among those mentioned that requires an associate degree level of training. Once school is complete, our training is never over. Medicine changes. New technology and research emerge that change best practices, and we are required to stay on top of that.

My certification expires every two years, and we are required to complete forty-eight to seventy-two hours of continuing education training and potentially retest depending on the state's requirements. To become a police officer or a firefighter, the training is generally a six-month academy, and while they do some continuing education, in most cases, their certifications do not expire. While there are subtle changes, the jobs pretty much stay the same. I have been out of the fire side for several years now, and I could theoretically jump right back on the truck if I wanted. You can't do that in EMS. So why are we so vastly underpaid compared to our peers when the level of training and upkeep is so much greater and the service we provide is so vital? I guess that's a question for the ages.

CHAPTER 14

THE SHELL CRACKS

Twice in my life, I have pondered suicide. However, I would not have considered myself suicidal. I thought about it in the way I think a lot of people think about it. Could I do it? How would I do it? Would I have the guts? What would my family think? But those were just fleeting thoughts with no real risk of doing it.

The first time I seriously considered it was after the death of my son. I wanted so badly to be reunited with him that, for a moment, I went through a full physical rehearsal. I walked to the room that contained my gun safe, unlocked it, and pondered the options. The pistol is the easiest. You just put it to your head and pull the trigger, but it's also the least powerful. It fires the smallest projectile at the slowest speed and carries the most risk of leaving you alive as a vegetable. I did not want to be stuck in a bed, being fed through a tube, and unable to wipe my own butt.

I moved on to the rifle. It fires the projectile at the highest speed but is big and clunky and could hurt someone else. That bullet can go through walls. The third option was the shotgun. It is also cumbersome but fires multiple projectiles, obliterating the target. It also doesn't run the risk of penetrating drywall and hitting someone else and was the most likely to complete the objective. I have never seen someone survive a shotgun wound. *That would probably be best,* I thought to my-self.

I pulled it from the safe, loaded a single round of 12-gauge 00 buckshot into it, and proceeded downstairs where I sat down on my piano bench. I sat there for a moment and mentally rehearsed the act. How would it go? Would I feel it? Would I go to Heaven? Do I believe in Heaven? I was still wrestling with my Chick-Fil-A epiphany. Would I get to see my boy again? My heart began to beat faster. I stared at the cold, blue steel protruding from between my shaking legs and pondered how I would manage to pull the trigger while staying on target.

I've seen people pull it with their toe. I removed my shoe. Now the logistics were resolved, there wasn't much left to do but to do it, but I wasn't ready yet. I sat there for a few moments, taking in the scene around me. I stared at the front door and imagined a scene playing out in front of me. Emily and Caia were returning from the grocery store, carrying the plastic bags into the kitchen. I was in a side room, so they probably wouldn't notice me at first. Emily might yell for me and ask me to come downstairs and help. I wouldn't respond, so she would probably assume I was asleep and come up to find me, only to realize that I was not there.

As she came down the stairs, she would be facing my body and see me there. I imagined the grotesque scenes I had responded to where the head had disappeared, brain matter splattered on the wall behind the poor soul who had decided enough was enough. Some of these folks probably had this same thought because they had taken such precautions as to encase themselves in plastic so as not to ruin the paint or upholstery of the chair to make it easier on the family. In every one of those scenes, I had considered what a ridiculous effort that was as I watched the devastation play out for the poor family members who had found them. In hopelessness, they believed the décor was more valuable than their own existence to the people that loved them, but those family members would have burned the place to the ground if it meant bringing them back. Now it was too late for that.

I pondered the permanence of death and the hole that was left in the lives of their loved ones, and how counterproductive and futile all of that was. How would Emily react when she saw my limp body, head blown apart, or worse…how would Caia react? How could I burden her with that image for the rest of her life? My wife had just lost her son, and my daughter, her brother. How could I even think of adding another layer to their pain just to end my own? And worse, where would it stop? Would they feel the need to follow my path? I couldn't do it. I put my shoe back on, unloaded the gun, and replaced it in the safe, and with that, my suicide rehearsal was over.

The second time was much different. It wasn't a singular event like the first time, but an all-consuming thought. A voice lingered in the back of my head, always prepared to reveal itself in a moment of weakness. I wasn't in control. It wasn't tangible like the shotgun had been. I couldn't decide to put it away. It was just there, like the Devil on my shoulder whispering in my ear. "Maybe you'd be better off dead," it would say.

This was the product of hopelessness, pure exhaustion, dissatisfaction, anger, and constant stress. When you put those together, they equal burnout. At first I would push it to the back of my mind and dismiss it as a ridiculous thought. "I'm tired, not suicidal," I'd tell myself.

Beep! "Sick person. Patient states that they don't feel well," chirped the radio.

"Really? It's three o'clock in the morning, and I haven't been to bed yet, and you call me for this?"

"Maybe you'd be better off dead," the voice whispered.

Get out of my head. No, I wouldn't.

"But maybe you would."

The occurrences increased and for more trivial reasons. One day, on the way back from the hospital, my partner rambled on and on about something. I wasn't even listening except to give him the occasional, "Uh huh," out of polite obligation. I couldn't concentrate on writing my report.

Man, I wish he would shut up, I thought to myself.

"If you were dead, you wouldn't have to listen him anymore," interjected the voice.

I barely noticed it this time. It had been popping up with such frequency, it was ingrained now. COVID raged on, and job dissatisfaction increased. I became more irritable as my irregular sleep patterns continued to take their toll on my body. Leadership ignored my requests and demands for intercession in whatever way they could to relieve the growing burdens being placed on us, and then demanded additional compliance with their policies, as if they had not heard me at all.

I had been bringing work home for a long time, but I just couldn't turn it off anymore. One day, in a fit of irritability, I started an argument with Emily. I don't even know what it was about, but I remember saying something like, "I wish I could just go to sleep and not wake up."

"What are you saying?" she asked. "That you are suicidal?"

It jarred me. I had given the voice a medium and said it out loud for the first time. *Yeah, I guess I am,* I thought. For months I had been arguing with this entity telling me it would be best if I didn't exist, but in a single spoken phrase,

I realized that voice had been my own all along. It scared me. I had gone from arguing with it to agreeing with it, and if I didn't seek help, I feared I might listen to it.

It was two manifestations of one idea. One scenario had me with a loaded shotgun in my hands, but the thing that scared me more was I had come to accept a thought I had once dismissed. In my career, I have responded to many suicides. In nearly every case, it came as a shock to those that knew the person best. If I had done the unthinkable in the months following Brayden's death, folks might have said, "Yeah, that makes sense. I probably couldn't have gone on either."

Many people expressed those very sentiments to me. They told me they didn't know how I continued and how much they admired my courage, and I would shrug and say, "What choice do I have?"

But when was the last time that you heard someone say, "It was only a matter of time," after someone took their own life? It's because the internal dialogue is deeply personal most of the time, and I believe those who are serious feel shame at the very notion of ending it all, but somehow can't bear the thought of going on either. The moment with the shotgun in my hands could have been where this led, but the months of thought, dialogue, and rationalization had not yet taken place, which is why I did not have the ability to go through with it. At some point though, in every victim's story, I believe this dialogue existed, and when the shotgun moment came, there was nothing left to consider. They had already completed the rationalization and done the work, so there was nothing between them and their fate.

My point is you rarely see it coming, and in my case, I didn't even realize I was in the weeds until I was already out. This epiphany settled in on me in November 2020 when a firefighter I had worked with briefly took a trip with friends. They went out to dinner, and then returned to their hotel rooms with plans to meet again the next day. When he didn't show up, they became concerned and knocked on the door of his room. He didn't answer, so they notified the hotel and the authorities who opened the door to find he had shot himself.

By all accounts, this came out of nowhere. He seemed genuinely happy, was well liked, had some good things going for him, and lit up the room when he walked in. While his shuffle walk in Crocs was a bit comical, he was outgoing and enjoyed cooking for the fire family, frequently bringing in crockpots filled with homemade concoctions to feed the boys, sometimes even on his off days. It took us all by surprise, but then, it always does. I wondered how long he had been bat-tling the inner dialogue. With his memory still fresh in my mind, and now that I had admitted what I had been denying, the next day I made an appointment with my doctor and voiced my concerns and was started on an anti-depressant. Was a job worth this?

"I guess when I don't love it anymore." I barely even heard those words when Billy said them to me all those years ago. They had almost no meaning to me back then. As far as I was concerned, Billy would never retire because it was impossible to grow tired of this career I had come to love so much. I stored the advice away with the words of my EMT instructor who advised me to document each call well because I wouldn't remember the call I ran last night, let alone the call I ran two or three years ago when I would be called upon the stand to testify in court. It seemed so outlandish that I would witness people dying and not recall it the next day, but I learned that lesson early.

I often leave the hospital and struggle to recall what the previous call was for, and if I get six to seven reports behind, you can forget about it. As the years have gone by, I have learned future me appreciates reminders from past me. I jot notes on the back of EKG paper that serve as memory triggers. They say things like, "55 yo tall AA m, spoke creole, CC CP. EKG normal. Vitals 110/85. HR 111. SpO2 97%. 20 g IV est R AC NS Lock Flush. 324 mg ASA, 0.4 mg NTG Adm. No improvement. Hospital X. Picked up in the red house with the old bulldog."

Some of these scribblings are shorthand medical terms, and some are just context clues to jog my memory. If I didn't write these notes, I would never re-member anything. It took me a lot longer to learn from Billy's wisdom, but through the years, his words have had time to rattle around in my head and have increased in amplitude with each call. "I guess when I don't love it anymore," I say to myself out loud sometimes.

Do I still love it? I used to derive pleasure from completion of a difficult skill, an attaboy from a doctor, the respect of my peers, or a report of a positive patient outcome, but more and more lately, I shrug those things off, and the frus-tration, exhaustion, and all the other negative thoughts have entrenched themselves in my mind and tipped the scale in the other direction. This is the hallmark of burnout and PTSD.

The landscape is littered with the scars of my past calls. I can't drive through my city without seeing the bark knocked off the tree where a car impacted it, killing two of its passengers. I think about them each and every time I pass it. I couldn't transport a patient to the hospital where my son was pronounced dead without seeing his limp head flop back in the room he was in. In many ways, our ghosts still dwell in that room, and I re-watch the experience as a spectator each time I walk by. I can't receive a call from an unknown number without my heart stopping and remembering the words of the police officer who gave me the news that day. I can't take a walk in the park without remembering the man who was just so done with life that one night he walked out to the end of the pier, looked out over the river shimmering with the glow of the lights from the other side, took a deep breath, and added his blood to the rising tide.

I am weathered by these experiences, these calls, these horrific memories, the death and broken bodies, the sleep deprivation, the nonsense, the abuse from patients, the administrative indifference, the years without proper vacations, the missed kids' baseball games and holidays, practicing medicine that is more influenced by the legal system and bureaucracy than the science, and being a cog in a broken system everyone knows is broken and nobody has any real solutions for. Some of these have eroded me over time, like sand blown in the wind or water over rocks. Some hit like a baseball bat, and others like a dump truck. Each one takes a little more of me, and in time, I've just gotten tired.

The nonsense, the run of the mill, and the day to day all cause burnout, but this is the type of burnout we can come back from. One of the good calls shows up and reinvigorates us for a time. We take a day off and get a little extra sleep. We do those wellness suggestions from HR to work out, eat right, get more sleep, get a massage, etc., and that's good enough to get by for a while longer, but then here come the baseball bats and the dump trucks. Somehow those HR suggestions just don't seem to meet the burden for those moments. It takes more sleep, more of the good calls where we can actually make a difference, and more time away to get through those. As for the dump trucks, sometimes you just can't leap that fence again.

My dump truck was the death of my son. In retrospect, that was the time I should have left the street, particularly after my altercation with the drunk lady. What I did not know was the experience of losing my own child had caused me so much pain and so much grief I was incapable of recognizing the rising temperature on my burnout meter. I liken it to the parable about boiling a frog. I am sure you have heard it, but if you have not, then I will fill you in. If you put a frog into boiling water, he will immediately jump out because his body recognizes the temperature is too hot and forces him out of the pot. If you place him into a room temperature pot and increase the heat gradually, he will remain in the pot until he boils to death because he does not recognize the danger he is in. That was me.

Once I had endured pain so great as the loss of my son, it was difficult for me to find empathy for others' pain or to recognize the rising temperature around me. The time away from the job and the support of my coworkers lured me into a false sense of healing and extended my career for another year. When that year brought me back to another low point, I ran away again and changed jobs in hopes of gaining more sleep, less abuse, and fewer calls. I found relief for a while longer, and again, my career was extended. All the while, the storm blown sand and baseball bats continued to grind away at me, but in my mind, I was still good.

What I didn't take account of was the grief and guilt I felt from leaving my Portsmouth family who were such a rock for me during those hard times. It was a catch twenty-two. I left the misery but lost the support system, and even though I did gain a few good friends along the way, a few of which I still consider family to this day, I never found what I had again. In my mind, this was just a job now, and there weren't the brotherly practical jokes and the history of humorous calls to reminisce about with my new group. It was less enjoyable, but the lower call volume made it manageable, and the occasional good call still brought me back over the fence again.

After nearly five years of trying to sort through our feelings, Emily and I decided the time was right to move and leave the grief-soaked landscape in the rearview mirror as we departed for Indiana. There would be no more guilt from driving past the cemetery without stopping or unpleasant flashbacks in haunted hospital rooms. It was a foolproof plan to shed our demons and start fresh. It *was* good for us, but in a sense, it was running again. With this move, I started a job with a new fire department that was busier with a more violent and more abusive population. I gained back all of the bullshit, more administrative indifference, and more of all of the things I ran from when I changed jobs the first time. And then COVID hit and cranked the volume to ten. Dump truck number two.

CHAPTER 15

YOU CAN'T RUN

After nearly five years away from the urban environment and a move halfway across the country, I convinced myself I was ready to return to the urban EMS environment. For the first year after the move, I worked for a private ambulance service that contracted with cities to deliver 911 service in addition to the interfacility transport services that was their bread and butter. I felt my experience and skills were wasted on the transport trucks, and I just did not enjoy that line of work, so I wasted no time in finding my way back onto a 911 truck.

The problem is when private service is combined with government service, we are operating under two different sets of rules whose individual interests often conflict with each other. This causes rifts between organizations and a high level of dissatisfaction for all involved. I also learned my employer had a poor reputation in the area, and with their name on my chest, I instantly gained their reputation and all the rights and privileges, or lack thereof, that came with it. I was used to people giving me respect and being comfortable in the knowledge I knew what I was doing, but here I was just another private service medic that wasn't held to the same standards the firefighters saw themselves being held to, and I wouldn't last as far as they were concerned. My interactions with them were short, strained, and I often found my decisions in question.

It came to a head one afternoon when the lieutenant on the engine walked up to me and reported our patient was a frequent flyer who is "always full of shit and there ain't nothing wrong with her today either."

"Okay," I replied, trusting his word but intent on verifying as I always do.

As I walked through the door, I immediately recognized there was more

159

to this patient than had been relayed. She was breathing rapidly, at almost double the normal rate, and was speaking in two- or three-word sentences. She didn't even have the breath to finish a sentence.

"Do you want to just give her a breathing treatment and see if you can get a refusal?" asked the lieutenant.

I looked at him, puzzled. Was there another patient here I was not seeing? It became clear to me his previous experiences with her had biased his judgement, and he was ignoring the obvious signs of distress as a result.

"No, I want to get her out to the truck where I can work," I replied curtly.

"Your call," he said, holding his hands up in surrender.

As we loaded her into the truck, I noticed nobody had gotten in with me except my partner who had joined me on this page. Evidently they weren't reading the same book. I listened to the patient's lungs, which was unnecessary because I could hear the unmistakable sound of fluid rattling around in them without a stethoscope. Sure enough, I found they were full of fluid. She was drowning in her own secretions.

I asked my partner for the CPAP device, a special mask that applies constant oxygen pressure to the tiny air sacs in the lungs and keeps them open for more efficient oxygen and carbon dioxide exchange. We were making headway, and the patient's oxygen levels began to improve. Suddenly, the backdoor opened again, and the lieutenant poked his head into the back to find out why we had not moved. He was surprised to see I had placed her on the CPAP mask.

"You pap'd her? Why?" he asked.

"She needed it," I replied, irritated at his complete inability to see past his own biases. He rolled his eyes and slammed the door.

Days later, my partner told me he had approached her and wanted to know "what my deal was." He told her I seemed like I didn't know what I was doing, and I got all spun up over nothing.

"He's a damn good medic, and that patient was going into respiratory failure," she defended me. "I'm learning a lot from him."

Over the next month, it became clear this incident had really gotten under his skin because she was approached multiple times by several different people who said he had told them I was a bad medic, a typical private service medic. "He won't last here."

As the saying goes, telephone, tell a friend, tell a fireman. In one call, my reputation in this department had been completely busted because one cocky lieutenant got his ego bruised. I had done nothing wrong. In fact, I had done everything right in spite of him, but that didn't stop the rumors from swirling. With time, I continued to prove I was highly skilled and knowledgeable, and others dismissed his criticisms as "typical of him," but because of this incident, my climb was so much steeper than it had to be, and it was all because of the name on my chest.

I hated working for a company that offered so little in the way of reputation. In addition, the pay wasn't great, the training was nonexistent, and they offered no retirement or paid vacation or sick days. This was the most dead-end job I had ever had, and I began to realize I was going to have to look to the city to gain any of those things back. Was I ready to handle urban EMS again though? Could I take it mentally? Could I endure the long sleepless nights, the impoverished demographics, and all the shootings, stabbings, overdoses, and abuses that come with them? I wasn't sure, but there was only one way to find out.

I applied to the Pike Township Fire Department and was offered the position. The offer letter was misleading. It listed a pay rate that was comparable to what I was making but failed to mention it came with substantial pay increases over three years, any paid sick or vacation days, and indicated I was eligible to participate in the public retirement plan but would not be vested for ten years, which seemed obscene to me. Furthermore, the department's leadership team was entirely composed of firefighters, and there was no opportunity for advancement of civilian EMS. I would be destined to be stuck as a street medic for the remainder of my career. It was Thursday, and I asked the HR director if I could have the weekend to think about it. "Of course," she replied.

Friday morning I reported to work, and we were scheduled to have a meeting with the CEO of the company to discuss the poor morale in the area. It was presented as a time for us to voice our concerns and for him to listen and take notes so he could make changes, but it started poorly when he failed to show up. Many employees had come in on their day off to participate, and when we called the dispatch office to find out where he was, we were told he had not even left headquarters yet, which was almost forty-five minutes away.

When he finally arrived, he was over two hours late, and most of the off-duty folks had gone home. His opening line was, "Sorry I'm late, but I promise you I'm worth the wait." I was immediately put off. He spent the next hour talking instead of listening, and when he finally opened the floor for questions, he informed us he knew we would complain about the pay, but he couldn't do anything about it because he was in the process of opening an ambulance manufacturing company that would make him millions, so he couldn't afford to pay any more right now. Then he put a period on it with the phrase, "So don't bother."

He followed up with, "Any other concerns?" I had some, but my decision was made in that meeting. I was taking the new job, so anything I had to say now was irrelevant. Urban EMS and all other concerns be damned, I wasn't working for this jerk anymore. I didn't wait. I got up, left the meeting, called the HR director from the hallway, accepted the position, and turned in my resignation before I pulled out of the parking lot, effective one day short of a full year of employment.

Things started well. I was immediately assigned to the busiest ambulance in the department and quickly got back into the flow of sleepless nights and missed meals. For a few months, I endured the baseball bats and storm blown sands, but I was getting tired already. Then one day we were dispatched to a local reservoir for the report of a drowning. Bystanders reported the man had been knocked off the boat by a large gust of wind, and despite his girlfriend's efforts to save him, he sank and didn't resurface.

I sat on standby for hours while the dive team looked for him. After thirty minutes of searching, the rescue attempt transitioned into a recovery, and the teams returned to shore to reorganize and develop a plan to grid search the water. Within minutes of the pause, the man's mother arrived and frantically searched the grounds for her son, but obviously did not find him. When she saw his friends, she demanded to know where he was, and all they could muster was, "In the water."

"What do you mean he's in the water? Why ain't nobody looking for him?" she screamed.

She had missed it all, just as I had missed it all in the hospital room that day. She couldn't accept this and decided to take matters into her own hands, set on sinking herself into the lake, before she was wrapped up by her husband and dragged away from the water's edge. She made a feeble attempt at resistance, but he wouldn't let her go, and finally, she resigned herself to what had happened. From deep in her stomach lurched the unmistakable, guttural wail of a mother who had lost her child. It caught in my throat, and in that moment, I found myself back in the hospital room standing over my dead son. I could almost feel the wind escaping from my own lungs, primal and uncontrollable. How much longer could I continue to do this? I had begun to break.

Still, the storm blown sands and baseball bats continued. Yellow toenails. Sand. Dead child. Baseball bat. Overdose, gunshot wound, overdose, drunk. Sand, sand, sand, sand. It was exhausting, but I had begun to notice I was deriving little pleasure or sense of accomplishment from the "good" calls anymore. It was harder to fall asleep, impossible to stay asleep, and difficult to wake up when I needed to.

Conversations with my wife transitioned from discussion about the interesting calls of the day to just me complaining about everything, something I had never done. I became exceedingly irritable toward my kids and developed a "don't like it, then fire me" attitude toward my job, all the while begging them to reconsider their leave policy or create some sort of advancement ladder that would get me off the street. Still, they shrugged. For the first time in my life, I had the thought, *Maybe I'd be better off dead.* Then I had it for the second time, and the third time, and then suddenly I couldn't get it out of my head. It wasn't until I said it out loud to my wife I realized just how often it had begun to permeate my thoughts.

COVID continued to rage on. Political protests, riots, and arguments broke out everywhere. Cops were getting shot simply for being cops, and public ire began to be directed toward Fire and EMS as well. The demand for our services was ever increasing and I had just had enough. Billy's words began to resonate louder and louder in my head. "I guess when I don't love it anymore."

I noticed things began to manifest physically for me as well. One afternoon, while sitting in a recliner at work, I felt short of breath. Taking my pulse, I found my heart was racing well above normal. I thought maybe I was just getting sick, but after it occurred a few more times in various settings, I realized I was experiencing the symptoms of anxiety. I didn't even need a trigger anymore. Everything was a trigger when you're constantly immersed in it. Now, 800 miles from where it all began, I realized that no matter how far I ran, I would never be able to get away. I needed to face it.

Chapter 16

Never Get Distracted

My grandfather asked me an age old ethical dilemma once. If you have two people with identical life threatening injuries, how do you decide which one to save? It's a twist on the paradigm of the out-of-control train in which your train is barreling toward five unsuspecting people. If you do nothing, then all five will die, but if you throw the switch and redirect the train, it will change direction and kill only one person. The catch is you will be responsible for the death of the one if you save the five, but if you do nothing, then you aren't responsible for the death of anyone, and their demise is simply an unavoidable tragedy.

The part that is often left out in the "do-nothing" scenario is doing nothing is a decision in and of itself. You are still culpable one way or another. I didn't even hesitate when my grandfather posed the question. "The younger one," I responded confidently. He seemed alarmed at my decisiveness.

"How do you make that determination?" he asked.

"It's simple," I responded. "You save the one with the most life left to live."

He thought for a moment and finally nodded his head. "That makes sense, I suppose."

Our general philosophy is to do the most good for the most people, and there is only so much of us to go around. Hypothetical philosophical debates are wonderful in the vacuum of a fantasy world where there are no lasting consequences. In the real world, our decisions have impact that may alter or end a person's life, cost a mother her child, or leave us debating our decisions for the rest of our lives.

Our training attempts to put these decisions on autopilot. It is almost algorithmic. We drill these scenarios repeatedly to mitigate the uncertainty when the real thing happens. In every scenario from EMT school on, invariably there will be a grotesque injury, such as a femur fracture with the bone sticking out of the leg. The scenario is designed to distract you from a much more sinister life threating injury if you spend too much time worried about the leg, such as the bullet wound in the chest if you fail to expose the torso, or a person lying unconscious in the ditch if you become hyper-focused on the leg patient. There is always something more to find.

To provide further distraction, the proctors may throw in a family member who won't leave you alone during the scenario or a set of vitals designed to lead you down a wild goose chase. The goal is to teach you to take a step back and make big picture decisions and not be so narrowly focused that you miss the important stuff. It is supposed to be second nature, and for the most part it is.

Our triage system is designed to funnel the worst patients into our care first and shed the distractions. Upon walking up to a mass casualty incident, we might scream out, "If you can hear me and you can walk, walk toward me!" This will clear the non-life threatening injuries and allow us to narrow our focus to the more severely injured. From there, we go one by one, treating immediate life threats and moving on after tagging them black, red, yellow, or green. This is the color-coding system used to separate the worst from those who will be fine for a while. Black means dead. Red means critically injured and needs more help than we can offer in the field. Yellow means serious but not life threatening, and green means walking wounded. This is all great in practice, but to put it into action in real life is something in which you can never adequately prepare for.

It was late at night and the bell alerted us for a vehicle accident. The notes read, "Car is inverted and on fire. Occupant trapped inside. Multiple calls." The multiple calls aspect of that information chain is what really got my blood flowing. People think steam pouring from the radiator means the car is on fire all the time. Airbag dust can also give this impression, so it is not uncommon for us to be alerted to a vehicle on fire, only to arrive and find it is not. The multiple calls addition changes that. This almost always means the notes are correct.

As we arrived, I found one car on its roof with flames shooting fifteen feet into the air from under the hood. As I approached the scene, I could see the occupant writhing around inside and the flames licking at them as they squirmed to escape into the backseat. I could smell the acrid stench of burning flesh and hair, a nauseating odor one never forgets. Everything in me wanted to run to that car and snatch them out, but I fought to calm myself and keep the big picture in mind. Realistically, there was nothing I could do for that person.

The car was on fire, I had no fire gear or water, and I was on the medic. My job was to render patient care, not make daring rescues, and there was a fire engine right behind me who was fully equipped and capable of doing what needed to be done for her. Learning to trust your team and realizing you are one cog in the machine is one of the hardest pieces of the job to learn. Everyone has a job, and experience is the only way you learn to analyze the situation and find your role. The cavalry was coming. By the time they got her out, there would be another medic there, so where should I be right now, in this moment?

Glancing around the scene, I realized there was a second car, so I put on my blinders, walked past the burning occupant, and scanned for secondary patients. It didn't take long to find some. The first I came to was a man lying on the ground with a cop on top of him doing CPR. "Does he have a pulse?" I asked.

He stopped for a moment and put his fingers to the man's neck. "No," he said.

"Then leave him. He's dead," I ordered. The cop didn't need to be told twice and jumped off him.

Next to the man was a lady, unconscious and moaning. I reached down to feel her pulse at the wrist but couldn't find one. I pressed my fingers into her neck and could feel only the faintest beat. This was an indication her blood pressure was extremely low. My partner came up behind me and asked me what I needed. "She's a red tag. We need to go," I informed her.

As I prepped my patient for departure, a cop tapped me on the shoulder and told me there was another patient. "What's wrong with them?" I asked.

"I don't know. I think maybe she hurt her leg or something, but she seems fine. She's walking around."

"Then she can wait," I told her.

Turning my attention back to my patient, I asked the cops for help loading her into the ambulance while my partner went to check on the other patient. As we moved toward the ambulance, the second medic arrived on scene and asked me what I had. "Two red, one black, one possible green. Yours is the one in the burning car as soon as they get her out." He nodded, and we proceeded to the truck.

In the back of the ambulance, the patient started to regain consciousness and became mildly combative as she realized she was strapped to a hard plastic board in an unfamiliar place. I did my best to calm her by explaining the situation. "You were in a bad accident, ma'am. You're hurt pretty badly, and we're going to take you to the hospital."

"I'm not hurt!" she screamed. "Where is my husband?"

I guessed the dead man was her husband but letting her know that wouldn't benefit either one of us at that moment. "I'm not sure," I lied. "There's a lot of folks taking care of people out there, and I'm sure he's in good hands."

She seemed to lose interest for the moment and began to calm down again. I cut her clothes off to search for those hidden injuries the instructors liked to throw at us. So far there was nothing obvious, but I needed to get to the bottom of her blood pressure, which was now confirmed at a dangerously low 60/22.

As I conducted my trauma assessment, she seemingly returned to a state of unconsciousness, and I moved my hands from head to chest, abdomen, and then to hips. As I pressed into her hips, she recoiled and awakened from her coma with a startling, shrill scream. Found it. A pelvic fracture can cause a person to bleed out rapidly into their abdomen, and you'd never see a drop of blood. That was my cue to get moving. We would later learn her injuries were much more complex.

To this day, it wrenches my gut to think about the person burning in the car I consciously decided to walk past, even while knowing the decision to do so may have saved another person's life. I know it was the right decision, but the guilt hasn't left me. The fact is, when it comes to my job, I am good at keeping the big picture in mind and ignoring the distractions when they are blood and guts, but I am not so good at it when it comes to taking care of myself. I don't think that many of us in this field are.

It is easy to get distracted by the most pressing matter in front of us and to get bogged down by the distractions, becoming tunnel focused on the crisis we perceive. All the while, there in the background, are parts of us desperately needing attention that are being neglected while we worry about something we can't change or just need to let someone else handle. Maybe we would all do a little better to keep the big picture in mind.

CHAPTER 17

NEW BEGINNINGS

I struggled with how I would end this book. I told you in the beginning that good writing begins with the end in mind, but that was difficult to do when I didn't know what I wanted to be when I grew up. As I wrote, it went through several different evolutions. It started as a journal that was supposed to be for my eyes only, but that was just a lot of complaining not even I wanted to read, so I scrapped some of that and added a few solutions to what was left.

Once I realized it was becoming a book, I added some anecodotes, and it evolved into a memoir, and as I dealt with my burnout, it maybe became a bit self-helpish, but that was never the intention. In the end, all I really wanted was to tell my story and shine a light into a job a lot of people really don't understand. I wanted to give you a peek into my most personal thoughts and feelings in a world where the default is to hide them, and I wanted to tell you exactly the kind of amazing people I have had the pleasure of serving with.

The only thing I know for certain is that it is time to change the scenery and pass the torch on to the next generation of paramedics. This time, I am not running though. This time, I am growing from a place of true healing. I want things to be better for them than they were for me. I want someone to take them seriously when they say they are tired and need a break. I want EMS to progress to the point where it is taken seriously as a profession and not just a pitstop for kids in search of an adrenaline rush. And I want us to do better for ourselves because who will if we don't?

I went through a phase where I thought I would leave EMS with a big outstretched middle finger to all the bad leadership, personal slights, and frustrations that come with the job, but in retrospect, this book has allowed me to sort through a lot of my feelings about the subject and put things into perspective. Who was I kidding anyway? I only know one thing and there isn't a huge market in the real world for people who specialize in bodily fluid management.

Looking back, it wasn't so bad. The friends I've made along the way have become family and that made all the difference. The support they gave me through the worst of times could never be repaid, but they didn't do it for that. They did it because I was one of them and will always be one of them. I now have clarity, and I think it would be a crying shame to turn my back on my family, old, new, and yet to come. My time on the street is coming to an end and I am happy to hand over the torch to eager young folks with a lot to learn, but I've got a lot of wisdom and experience to share with them.

This book is only the first chapter of my contribution to that end. I have decided to hang around in a leadership role and be better where my leadership fell short. I did have a great role model, after all. I wouldn't be where I am without the mentorship of people like Boz and the rest of the greats that have appeared so often throughout this book. It's time for me to be that for the next generation.

So for those of you coming on, enjoy the good times and don't take them for granted. Give your all and be the best you can be, because some day, someone's mother will need you to be better than the best. Be aware of your own mind, listen when it tells you that you need help, and *never* be afraid to ask for it. This job is hard, miserable at times, and it takes a lot of you with it. But it also gives back a lot too. Do great things. As for me, here's to sleeping nights, holidays with the family, and new beginnings. I quit…sort of.

-"Captain" Chad A. Davis

EPILOGUE

This book got shelved for months while I tried to figure out which direction I was going. It was originally entitled *I Quit: The Things I Wish I Could Have Said When I Was a Paramedic*, and was going to be my resignation letter.

For a while it was really a crapshoot as to whether I would remain in EMS. I applied for several jobs outside the field, intent on starting anew, but as the months passed and no callbacks came, some of the burnout I was facing started to alleviate as COVID began to wane. I started thinking maybe I still had something to offer. So I began to apply for jobs in EMS leadership, but so many of them required progressive command experience, which as an eighteen-year grunt I had none, so I wasn't getting a lot of interest there either.

In the meantime, I got tired of having this book open on my desktop and decided I would finish it and if the ending needed to change, I'd change it. On the day I put what I believed to be the final period on it, I received a call back for a captain's job in Vermont. If you're not one to read the last chapter first, you know I am a believer, and I don't think it is any coincidence this book was completed just hours before the request for an interview came in. As a sidenote, within literally thirty seconds of being offered that job, I received a call from a publisher who wanted to publish the book. No coincidences here.

In one of the most unique interview processes I have ever been a part of, the leadership team invited the entire staff to lunch with me where they were given an open floor to ask anything they wished. There was no script, and nobody was recording my responses and nodding their heads in approval or disapproval. It was a raw, informal discussion. At first it was intimidating, but as the conversation progressed, it became clear as to why they do it this way, and I found it admirable the leadership team valued the input of the employees enough to allow them this opportunity.

Some of them asked questions they had heard in their own interviews. "How do you handle conflict?" "How important is physical fitness to you?" "Where do you see yourself in five years?" As it went on, it became more relaxed. "What do you do for fun?" "Do you like to hunt or fish?" "What's your favorite baseball team?" And then there was this one: "So I don't mean to be blunt or whatever, but how are you going to keep this from going to your head?"

The room laughed nervously, but I didn't. I appreciated the honesty and the guts it took to ask that of someone who would potentially be her supervisor. That is the kind of question every leader should have to answer before being placed in a position of leadership. It told me all I needed to know about that young lady's experiences with management and what her expectations were of me. It also gave me a real sense of what I was walking into and clues about where previous captains had failed. The answer I gave was nowhere near as detailed as the one I give now.

So to the person that asked that question, if you read this book, I hope you will see at heart, I am one of you. I am no stranger to sleepless nights, missed events with the family, and a healthy dose of bullshit runs. I have been mentored by the very best EMS has to offer and suffered under poor leadership at times. I believe leaders should see themselves as nothing more than servants to those they lead, and my job is to make yours easier. My biggest role model is a redneck with a mustache and a southern drawl. I hope you will see Boz in me and I will make an impact on you in the same way he did me. Let it be known, here and now, I've always got your back if you follow these three rules:

1. Always do what is right;
2. No horseplay;
3. Know your job and be ready to do it when the tone goes off.

If you do that, you'll have no problems with me. I hope that adequately answers your question.